C-2309 CAREER EXAMINATION SERIES

This is your
PASSBOOK for...

Medical Records Clerk

Test Preparation Study Guide
Questions & Answers

NATIONAL LEARNING CORPORATION ®

COPYRIGHT NOTICE

This book is SOLELY intended for, is sold ONLY to, and its use is RESTRICTED to individual, bona fide applicants or candidates who qualify by virtue of having seriously filed applications for appropriate license, certificate, professional and/or promotional advancement, higher school matriculation, scholarship, or other legitimate requirements of education and/or governmental authorities.

This book is NOT intended for use, class instruction, tutoring, training, duplication, copying, reprinting, excerption, or adaptation, etc., by:

1) Other publishers
2) Proprietors and/or Instructors of "Coaching" and/or Preparatory Courses
3) Personnel and/or Training Divisions of commercial, industrial, and governmental organizations
4) Schools, colleges, or universities and/or their departments and staffs, including teachers and other personnel
5) Testing Agencies or Bureaus
6) Study groups which seek by the purchase of a single volume to copy and/or duplicate and/or adapt this material for use by the group as a whole without having purchased individual volumes for each of the members of the group
7) Et al.

Such persons would be in violation of appropriate Federal and State statutes.

PROVISION OF LICENSING AGREEMENTS – Recognized educational, commercial, industrial, and governmental institutions and organizations, and others legitimately engaged in educational pursuits, including training, testing, and measurement activities, may address request for a licensing agreement to the copyright owners, who will determine whether, and under what conditions, including fees and charges, the materials in this book may be used them. In other words, a licensing facility exists for the legitimate use of the material in this book on other than an individual basis. However, it is asseverated and affirmed here that the material in this book CANNOT be used without the receipt of the express permission of such a licensing agreement from the Publishers. Inquiries re licensing should be addressed to the company, attention rights and permissions department.

All rights reserved, including the right of reproduction in whole or in part, in any form or by any means, electronic or mechanical, including photocopying, recording, or by any information storage and retrieval system, without permission in writing from the Publisher.

Copyright © 2025 by
National Learning Corporation

212 Michael Drive, Syosset, NY 11791
(516) 921-8888 • www.passbooks.com
E-mail: info@passbooks.com

PASSBOOK® SERIES

THE *PASSBOOK® SERIES* has been created to prepare applicants and candidates for the ultimate academic battlefield – the examination room.

At some time in our lives, each and every one of us may be required to take an examination – for validation, matriculation, admission, qualification, registration, certification, or licensure.

Based on the assumption that every applicant or candidate has met the basic formal educational standards, has taken the required number of courses, and read the necessary texts, the *PASSBOOK® SERIES* furnishes the one special preparation which may assure passing with confidence, instead of failing with insecurity. Examination questions – together with answers – are furnished as the basic vehicle for study so that the mysteries of the examination and its compounding difficulties may be eliminated or diminished by a sure method.

This book is meant to help you pass your examination provided that you qualify and are serious in your objective.

The entire field is reviewed through the huge store of content information which is succinctly presented through a provocative and challenging approach – the question-and-answer method.

A climate of success is established by furnishing the correct answers at the end of each test.

You soon learn to recognize types of questions, forms of questions, and patterns of questioning. You may even begin to anticipate expected outcomes.

You perceive that many questions are repeated or adapted so that you can gain acute insights, which may enable you to score many sure points.

You learn how to confront new questions, or types of questions, and to attack them confidently and work out the correct answers.

You note objectives and emphases, and recognize pitfalls and dangers, so that you may make positive educational adjustments.

Moreover, you are kept fully informed in relation to new concepts, methods, practices, and directions in the field.

You discover that you are actually taking the examination all the time: you are preparing for the examination by "taking" an examination, not by reading extraneous and/or supererogatory textbooks.

In short, this PASSBOOK®, used directedly, should be an important factor in helping you to pass your test.

MEDICAL RECORDS CLERK

DUTIES
Compiles and maintains medical records for a county department; performs related work as required.

SCOPE OF THE EXAMINATION
The written test will be designed to test for knowledge, skills, and/or abilities in such areas as:
1. Record keeping;
2. Following directions in the use of number-letter codes;
3. Understanding and interpreting written material;
4. Arithmetic reasoning; and
5. Medical terminology.

HOW TO TAKE A TEST

I. YOU MUST PASS AN EXAMINATION

A. WHAT EVERY CANDIDATE SHOULD KNOW

Examination applicants often ask us for help in preparing for the written test. What can I study in advance? What kinds of questions will be asked? How will the test be given? How will the papers be graded?

As an applicant for a civil service examination, you may be wondering about some of these things. Our purpose here is to suggest effective methods of advance study and to describe civil service examinations.

Your chances for success on this examination can be increased if you know how to prepare. Those "pre-examination jitters" can be reduced if you know what to expect. You can even experience an adventure in good citizenship if you know why civil service exams are given.

B. WHY ARE CIVIL SERVICE EXAMINATIONS GIVEN?

Civil service examinations are important to you in two ways. As a citizen, you want public jobs filled by employees who know how to do their work. As a job seeker, you want a fair chance to compete for that job on an equal footing with other candidates. The best-known means of accomplishing this two-fold goal is the competitive examination.

Exams are widely publicized throughout the nation. They may be administered for jobs in federal, state, city, municipal, town or village governments or agencies.

Any citizen may apply, with some limitations, such as the age or residence of applicants. Your experience and education may be reviewed to see whether you meet the requirements for the particular examination. When these requirements exist, they are reasonable and applied consistently to all applicants. Thus, a competitive examination may cause you some uneasiness now, but it is your privilege and safeguard.

C. HOW ARE CIVIL SERVICE EXAMS DEVELOPED?

Examinations are carefully written by trained technicians who are specialists in the field known as "psychological measurement," in consultation with recognized authorities in the field of work that the test will cover. These experts recommend the subject matter areas or skills to be tested; only those knowledges or skills important to your success on the job are included. The most reliable books and source materials available are used as references. Together, the experts and technicians judge the difficulty level of the questions.

Test technicians know how to phrase questions so that the problem is clearly stated. Their ethics do not permit "trick" or "catch" questions. Questions may have been tried out on sample groups, or subjected to statistical analysis, to determine their usefulness.

Written tests are often used in combination with performance tests, ratings of training and experience, and oral interviews. All of these measures combine to form the best-known means of finding the right person for the right job.

II. HOW TO PASS THE WRITTEN TEST

A. NATURE OF THE EXAMINATION

To prepare intelligently for civil service examinations, you should know how they differ from school examinations you have taken. In school you were assigned certain definite pages to read or subjects to cover. The examination questions were quite detailed and usually emphasized memory. Civil service exams, on the other hand, try to discover your present ability to perform the duties of a position, plus your potentiality to learn these duties. In other words, a civil service exam attempts to predict how successful you will be. Questions cover such a broad area that they cannot be as minute and detailed as school exam questions.

In the public service similar kinds of work, or positions, are grouped together in one "class." This process is known as *position-classification*. All the positions in a class are paid according to the salary range for that class. One class title covers all of these positions, and they are all tested by the same examination.

B. FOUR BASIC STEPS

1) Study the announcement

How, then, can you know what subjects to study? Our best answer is: "Learn as much as possible about the class of positions for which you've applied." The exam will test the knowledge, skills and abilities needed to do the work.

Your most valuable source of information about the position you want is the official exam announcement. This announcement lists the training and experience qualifications. Check these standards and apply only if you come reasonably close to meeting them.

The brief description of the position in the examination announcement offers some clues to the subjects which will be tested. Think about the job itself. Review the duties in your mind. Can you perform them, or are there some in which you are rusty? Fill in the blank spots in your preparation.

Many jurisdictions preview the written test in the exam announcement by including a section called "Knowledge and Abilities Required," "Scope of the Examination," or some similar heading. Here you will find out specifically what fields will be tested.

2) Review your own background

Once you learn in general what the position is all about, and what you need to know to do the work, ask yourself which subjects you already know fairly well and which need improvement. You may wonder whether to concentrate on improving your strong areas or on building some background in your fields of weakness. When the announcement has specified "some knowledge" or "considerable knowledge," or has used adjectives like "beginning principles of..." or "advanced ... methods," you can get a clue as to the number and difficulty of questions to be asked in any given field. More questions, and hence broader coverage, would be included for those subjects which are more important in the work. Now weigh your strengths and weaknesses against the job requirements and prepare accordingly.

3) Determine the level of the position

Another way to tell how intensively you should prepare is to understand the level of the job for which you are applying. Is it the entering level? In other words, is this the position in which beginners in a field of work are hired? Or is it an intermediate or advanced level? Sometimes this is indicated by such words as "Junior" or "Senior" in the class title. Other jurisdictions use Roman numerals to designate the level – Clerk I, Clerk II, for example. The word "Supervisor" sometimes appears in the title. If the level is not indicated by the title, check the description of duties. Will you be working under very close supervision, or will you have responsibility for independent decisions in this work?

4) Choose appropriate study materials

Now that you know the subjects to be examined and the relative amount of each subject to be covered, you can choose suitable study materials. For beginning level jobs, or even advanced ones, if you have a pronounced weakness in some aspect of your training, read a modern, standard textbook in that field. Be sure it is up to date and has general coverage. Such books are normally available at your library, and the librarian will be glad to help you locate one. For entry-level positions, questions of appropriate difficulty are chosen -- neither highly advanced questions, nor those too simple. Such questions require careful thought but not advanced training.

If the position for which you are applying is technical or advanced, you will read more advanced, specialized material. If you are already familiar with the basic principles of your field, elementary textbooks would waste your time. Concentrate on advanced textbooks and technical periodicals. Think through the concepts and review difficult problems in your field.

These are all general sources. You can get more ideas on your own initiative, following these leads. For example, training manuals and publications of the government agency which employs workers in your field can be useful, particularly for technical and professional positions. A letter or visit to the government department involved may result in more specific study suggestions, and certainly will provide you with a more definite idea of the exact nature of the position you are seeking.

III. KINDS OF TESTS

Tests are used for purposes other than measuring knowledge and ability to perform specified duties. For some positions, it is equally important to test ability to make adjustments to new situations or to profit from training. In others, basic mental abilities not dependent on information are essential. Questions which test these things may not appear as pertinent to the duties of the position as those which test for knowledge and information. Yet they are often highly important parts of a fair examination. For very general questions, it is almost impossible to help you direct your study efforts. What we can do is to point out some of the more common of these general abilities needed in public service positions and describe some typical questions.

1) General information

Broad, general information has been found useful for predicting job success in some kinds of work. This is tested in a variety of ways, from vocabulary lists to questions about current events. Basic background in some field of work, such as sociology or economics, may be sampled in a group of questions. Often these are principles which have become familiar to most persons through exposure rather than through formal training. It is difficult to advise you how to study for these questions; being alert to the world around you is our best suggestion.

2) Verbal ability

An example of an ability needed in many positions is verbal or language ability. Verbal ability is, in brief, the ability to use and understand words. Vocabulary and grammar tests are typical measures of this ability. Reading comprehension or paragraph interpretation questions are common in many kinds of civil service tests. You are given a paragraph of written material and asked to find its central meaning.

3) **Numerical ability**

Number skills can be tested by the familiar arithmetic problem, by checking paired lists of numbers to see which are alike and which are different, or by interpreting charts and graphs. In the latter test, a graph may be printed in the test booklet which you are asked to use as the basis for answering questions.

4) **Observation**

A popular test for law-enforcement positions is the observation test. A picture is shown to you for several minutes, then taken away. Questions about the picture test your ability to observe both details and larger elements.

5) **Following directions**

In many positions in the public service, the employee must be able to carry out written instructions dependably and accurately. You may be given a chart with several columns, each column listing a variety of information. The questions require you to carry out directions involving the information given in the chart.

6) **Skills and aptitudes**

Performance tests effectively measure some manual skills and aptitudes. When the skill is one in which you are trained, such as typing or shorthand, you can practice. These tests are often very much like those given in business school or high school courses. For many of the other skills and aptitudes, however, no short-time preparation can be made. Skills and abilities natural to you or that you have developed throughout your lifetime are being tested.

Many of the general questions just described provide all the data needed to answer the questions and ask you to use your reasoning ability to find the answers. Your best preparation for these tests, as well as for tests of facts and ideas, is to be at your physical and mental best. You, no doubt, have your own methods of getting into an exam-taking mood and keeping "in shape." The next section lists some ideas on this subject.

IV. KINDS OF QUESTIONS

Only rarely is the "essay" question, which you answer in narrative form, used in civil service tests. Civil service tests are usually of the short-answer type. Full instructions for answering these questions will be given to you at the examination. But in case this is your first experience with short-answer questions and separate answer sheets, here is what you need to know:

1) Multiple-choice Questions

Most popular of the short-answer questions is the "multiple choice" or "best answer" question. It can be used, for example, to test for factual knowledge, ability to solve problems or judgment in meeting situations found at work.

A multiple-choice question is normally one of three types—
- It can begin with an incomplete statement followed by several possible endings. You are to find the one ending which *best* completes the statement, although some of the others may not be entirely wrong.
- It can also be a complete statement in the form of a question which is answered by choosing one of the statements listed.

- It can be in the form of a problem – again you select the best answer.

Here is an example of a multiple-choice question with a discussion which should give you some clues as to the method for choosing the right answer:

When an employee has a complaint about his assignment, the action which will *best* help him overcome his difficulty is to
   A. discuss his difficulty with his coworkers
   B. take the problem to the head of the organization
   C. take the problem to the person who gave him the assignment
   D. say nothing to anyone about his complaint

In answering this question, you should study each of the choices to find which is best. Consider choice "A" – Certainly an employee may discuss his complaint with fellow employees, but no change or improvement can result, and the complaint remains unresolved. Choice "B" is a poor choice since the head of the organization probably does not know what assignment you have been given, and taking your problem to him is known as "going over the head" of the supervisor. The supervisor, or person who made the assignment, is the person who can clarify it or correct any injustice. Choice "C" is, therefore, correct. To say nothing, as in choice "D," is unwise. Supervisors have and interest in knowing the problems employees are facing, and the employee is seeking a solution to his problem.

2) True/False Questions

The "true/false" or "right/wrong" form of question is sometimes used. Here a complete statement is given. Your job is to decide whether the statement is right or wrong.

SAMPLE: A roaming cell-phone call to a nearby city costs less than a non-roaming call to a distant city.

This statement is wrong, or false, since roaming calls are more expensive.

This is not a complete list of all possible question forms, although most of the others are variations of these common types. You will always get complete directions for answering questions. Be sure you understand *how* to mark your answers – ask questions until you do.

V. RECORDING YOUR ANSWERS

Computer terminals are used more and more today for many different kinds of exams.

For an examination with very few applicants, you may be told to record your answers in the test booklet itself. Separate answer sheets are much more common. If this separate answer sheet is to be scored by machine – and this is often the case – it is highly important that you mark your answers correctly in order to get credit.

An electronic scoring machine is often used in civil service offices because of the speed with which papers can be scored. Machine-scored answer sheets must be marked with a pencil, which will be given to you. This pencil has a high graphite content which responds to the electronic scoring machine. As a matter of fact, stray dots may register as answers, so do not let your pencil rest on the answer sheet while you are pondering the correct answer. Also, if your pencil lead breaks or is otherwise defective, ask for another.

Since the answer sheet will be dropped in a slot in the scoring machine, be careful not to bend the corners or get the paper crumpled.

The answer sheet normally has five vertical columns of numbers, with 30 numbers to a column. These numbers correspond to the question numbers in your test booklet. After each number, going across the page are four or five pairs of dotted lines. These short dotted lines have small letters or numbers above them. The first two pairs may also have a "T" or "F" above the letters. This indicates that the first two pairs only are to be used if the questions are of the true-false type. If the questions are multiple choice, disregard the "T" and "F" and pay attention only to the small letters or numbers.

Answer your questions in the manner of the sample that follows:

32. The largest city in the United States is
    A. Washington, D.C.
    B. New York City
    C. Chicago
    D. Detroit
    E. San Francisco

1) Choose the answer you think is best. (New York City is the largest, so "B" is correct.)
2) Find the row of dotted lines numbered the same as the question you are answering. (Find row number 32)
3) Find the pair of dotted lines corresponding to the answer. (Find the pair of lines under the mark "B.")
4) Make a solid black mark between the dotted lines.

VI. BEFORE THE TEST

Common sense will help you find procedures to follow to get ready for an examination. Too many of us, however, overlook these sensible measures. Indeed, nervousness and fatigue have been found to be the most serious reasons why applicants fail to do their best on civil service tests. Here is a list of reminders:

- Begin your preparation early – Don't wait until the last minute to go scurrying around for books and materials or to find out what the position is all about.
- Prepare continuously – An hour a night for a week is better than an all-night cram session. This has been definitely established. What is more, a night a week for a month will return better dividends than crowding your study into a shorter period of time.
- Locate the place of the exam – You have been sent a notice telling you when and where to report for the examination. If the location is in a different town or otherwise unfamiliar to you, it would be well to inquire the best route and learn something about the building.
- Relax the night before the test – Allow your mind to rest. Do not study at all that night. Plan some mild recreation or diversion; then go to bed early and get a good night's sleep.
- Get up early enough to make a leisurely trip to the place for the test – This way unforeseen events, traffic snarls, unfamiliar buildings, etc. will not upset you.
- Dress comfortably – A written test is not a fashion show. You will be known by number and not by name, so wear something comfortable.

- Leave excess paraphernalia at home – Shopping bags and odd bundles will get in your way. You need bring only the items mentioned in the official notice you received; usually everything you need is provided. Do not bring reference books to the exam. They will only confuse those last minutes and be taken away from you when in the test room.
- Arrive somewhat ahead of time – If because of transportation schedules you must get there very early, bring a newspaper or magazine to take your mind off yourself while waiting.
- Locate the examination room – When you have found the proper room, you will be directed to the seat or part of the room where you will sit. Sometimes you are given a sheet of instructions to read while you are waiting. Do not fill out any forms until you are told to do so; just read them and be prepared.
- Relax and prepare to listen to the instructions
- If you have any physical problem that may keep you from doing your best, be sure to tell the test administrator. If you are sick or in poor health, you really cannot do your best on the exam. You can come back and take the test some other time.

VII. AT THE TEST

The day of the test is here and you have the test booklet in your hand. The temptation to get going is very strong. Caution! There is more to success than knowing the right answers. You must know how to identify your papers and understand variations in the type of short-answer question used in this particular examination. Follow these suggestions for maximum results from your efforts:

1) Cooperate with the monitor

The test administrator has a duty to create a situation in which you can be as much at ease as possible. He will give instructions, tell you when to begin, check to see that you are marking your answer sheet correctly, and so on. He is not there to guard you, although he will see that your competitors do not take unfair advantage. He wants to help you do your best.

2) Listen to all instructions

Don't jump the gun! Wait until you understand all directions. In most civil service tests you get more time than you need to answer the questions. So don't be in a hurry. Read each word of instructions until you clearly understand the meaning. Study the examples, listen to all announcements and follow directions. Ask questions if you do not understand what to do.

3) Identify your papers

Civil service exams are usually identified by number only. You will be assigned a number; you must not put your name on your test papers. Be sure to copy your number correctly. Since more than one exam may be given, copy your exact examination title.

4) Plan your time

Unless you are told that a test is a "speed" or "rate of work" test, speed itself is usually not important. Time enough to answer all the questions will be provided, but this does not mean that you have all day. An overall time limit has been set. Divide the total time (in minutes) by the number of questions to determine the approximate time you have for each question.

5) Do not linger over difficult questions

If you come across a difficult question, mark it with a paper clip (useful to have along) and come back to it when you have been through the booklet. One caution if you do this – be sure to skip a number on your answer sheet as well. Check often to be sure that you have not lost your place and that you are marking in the row numbered the same as the question you are answering.

6) Read the questions

Be sure you know what the question asks! Many capable people are unsuccessful because they failed to *read* the questions correctly.

7) Answer all questions

Unless you have been instructed that a penalty will be deducted for incorrect answers, it is better to guess than to omit a question.

8) Speed tests

It is often better NOT to guess on speed tests. It has been found that on timed tests people are tempted to spend the last few seconds before time is called in marking answers at random – without even reading them – in the hope of picking up a few extra points. To discourage this practice, the instructions may warn you that your score will be "corrected" for guessing. That is, a penalty will be applied. The incorrect answers will be deducted from the correct ones, or some other penalty formula will be used.

9) Review your answers

If you finish before time is called, go back to the questions you guessed or omitted to give them further thought. Review other answers if you have time.

10) Return your test materials

If you are ready to leave before others have finished or time is called, take ALL your materials to the monitor and leave quietly. Never take any test material with you. The monitor can discover whose papers are not complete, and taking a test booklet may be grounds for disqualification.

VIII. EXAMINATION TECHNIQUES

1) Read the general instructions carefully. These are usually printed on the first page of the exam booklet. As a rule, these instructions refer to the timing of the examination; the fact that you should not start work until the signal and must stop work at a signal, etc. If there are any *special* instructions, such as a choice of questions to be answered, make sure that you note this instruction carefully.

2) When you are ready to start work on the examination, that is as soon as the signal has been given, read the instructions to each question booklet, underline any key words or phrases, such as *least, best, outline, describe* and the like. In this way you will tend to answer as requested rather than discover on reviewing your paper that you *listed without describing*, that you selected the *worst* choice rather than the *best* choice, etc.

3) If the examination is of the objective or multiple-choice type – that is, each question will also give a series of possible answers: A, B, C or D, and you are called upon to select the best answer and write the letter next to that answer on your answer paper – it is advisable to start answering each question in turn. There may be anywhere from 50 to 100 such questions in the three or four hours allotted and you can see how much time would be taken if you read through all the questions before beginning to answer any. Furthermore, if you come across a question or group of questions which you know would be difficult to answer, it would undoubtedly affect your handling of all the other questions.

4) If the examination is of the essay type and contains but a few questions, it is a moot point as to whether you should read all the questions before starting to answer any one. Of course, if you are given a choice – say five out of seven and the like – then it is essential to read all the questions so you can eliminate the two that are most difficult. If, however, you are asked to answer all the questions, there may be danger in trying to answer the easiest one first because you may find that you will spend too much time on it. The best technique is to answer the first question, then proceed to the second, etc.

5) Time your answers. Before the exam begins, write down the time it started, then add the time allowed for the examination and write down the time it must be completed, then divide the time available somewhat as follows:
    - If 3-1/2 hours are allowed, that would be 210 minutes. If you have 80 objective-type questions, that would be an average of 2-1/2 minutes per question. Allow yourself no more than 2 minutes per question, or a total of 160 minutes, which will permit about 50 minutes to review.
    - If for the time allotment of 210 minutes there are 7 essay questions to answer, that would average about 30 minutes a question. Give yourself only 25 minutes per question so that you have about 35 minutes to review.

6) The most important instruction is to *read each question* and make sure you know what is wanted. The second most important instruction is to *time yourself properly* so that you answer every question. The third most important instruction is to *answer every question*. Guess if you have to but include something for each question. Remember that you will receive no credit for a blank and will probably receive some credit if you write something in answer to an essay question. If you guess a letter – say "B" for a multiple-choice question – you may have guessed right. If you leave a blank as an answer to a multiple-choice question, the examiners may respect your feelings but it will not add a point to your score. Some exams may penalize you for wrong answers, so in such cases *only*, you may not want to guess unless you have some basis for your answer.

7) Suggestions
    a. Objective-type questions
        1. Examine the question booklet for proper sequence of pages and questions
        2. Read all instructions carefully
        3. Skip any question which seems too difficult; return to it after all other questions have been answered
        4. Apportion your time properly; do not spend too much time on any single question or group of questions

5. Note and underline key words – *all, most, fewest, least, best, worst, same, opposite*, etc.
6. Pay particular attention to negatives
7. Note unusual option, e.g., unduly long, short, complex, different or similar in content to the body of the question
8. Observe the use of "hedging" words – *probably, may, most likely*, etc.
9. Make sure that your answer is put next to the same number as the question
10. Do not second-guess unless you have good reason to believe the second answer is definitely more correct
11. Cross out original answer if you decide another answer is more accurate; do not erase until you are ready to hand your paper in
12. Answer all questions; guess unless instructed otherwise
13. Leave time for review

b. Essay questions
  1. Read each question carefully
  2. Determine exactly what is wanted. Underline key words or phrases.
  3. Decide on outline or paragraph answer
  4. Include many different points and elements unless asked to develop any one or two points or elements
  5. Show impartiality by giving pros and cons unless directed to select one side only
  6. Make and write down any assumptions you find necessary to answer the questions
  7. Watch your English, grammar, punctuation and choice of words
  8. Time your answers; don't crowd material

8) Answering the essay question

Most essay questions can be answered by framing the specific response around several key words or ideas. Here are a few such key words or ideas:

M's: manpower, materials, methods, money, management
P's: purpose, program, policy, plan, procedure, practice, problems, pitfalls, personnel, public relations

  a. Six basic steps in handling problems:
    1. Preliminary plan and background development
    2. Collect information, data and facts
    3. Analyze and interpret information, data and facts
    4. Analyze and develop solutions as well as make recommendations
    5. Prepare report and sell recommendations
    6. Install recommendations and follow up effectiveness

  b. Pitfalls to avoid
    1. *Taking things for granted* – A statement of the situation does not necessarily imply that each of the elements is necessarily true; for example, a complaint may be invalid and biased so that all that can be taken for granted is that a complaint has been registered

2. *Considering only one side of a situation* – Wherever possible, indicate several alternatives and then point out the reasons you selected the best one
3. *Failing to indicate follow up* – Whenever your answer indicates action on your part, make certain that you will take proper follow-up action to see how successful your recommendations, procedures or actions turn out to be
4. *Taking too long in answering any single question* – Remember to time your answers properly

IX. AFTER THE TEST

Scoring procedures differ in detail among civil service jurisdictions although the general principles are the same. Whether the papers are hand-scored or graded by machine we have described, they are nearly always graded by number. That is, the person who marks the paper knows only the number – never the name – of the applicant. Not until all the papers have been graded will they be matched with names. If other tests, such as training and experience or oral interview ratings have been given, scores will be combined. Different parts of the examination usually have different weights. For example, the written test might count 60 percent of the final grade, and a rating of training and experience 40 percent. In many jurisdictions, veterans will have a certain number of points added to their grades.

After the final grade has been determined, the names are placed in grade order and an eligible list is established. There are various methods for resolving ties between those who get the same final grade – probably the most common is to place first the name of the person whose application was received first. Job offers are made from the eligible list in the order the names appear on it. You will be notified of your grade and your rank as soon as all these computations have been made. This will be done as rapidly as possible.

People who are found to meet the requirements in the announcement are called "eligibles." Their names are put on a list of eligible candidates. An eligible's chances of getting a job depend on how high he stands on this list and how fast agencies are filling jobs from the list.

When a job is to be filled from a list of eligibles, the agency asks for the names of people on the list of eligibles for that job. When the civil service commission receives this request, it sends to the agency the names of the three people highest on this list. Or, if the job to be filled has specialized requirements, the office sends the agency the names of the top three persons who meet these requirements from the general list.

The appointing officer makes a choice from among the three people whose names were sent to him. If the selected person accepts the appointment, the names of the others are put back on the list to be considered for future openings.

That is the rule in hiring from all kinds of eligible lists, whether they are for typist, carpenter, chemist, or something else. For every vacancy, the appointing officer has his choice of any one of the top three eligibles on the list. This explains why the person whose name is on top of the list sometimes does not get an appointment when some of the persons lower on the list do. If the appointing officer chooses the second or third eligible, the No. 1 eligible does not get a job at once, but stays on the list until he is appointed or the list is terminated.

X. HOW TO PASS THE INTERVIEW TEST

The examination for which you applied requires an oral interview test. You have already taken the written test and you are now being called for the interview test – the final part of the formal examination.

You may think that it is not possible to prepare for an interview test and that there are no procedures to follow during an interview. Our purpose is to point out some things you can do in advance that will help you and some good rules to follow and pitfalls to avoid while you are being interviewed.

What is an interview supposed to test?

The written examination is designed to test the technical knowledge and competence of the candidate; the oral is designed to evaluate intangible qualities, not readily measured otherwise, and to establish a list showing the relative fitness of each candidate – as measured against his competitors – for the position sought. Scoring is not on the basis of "right" and "wrong," but on a sliding scale of values ranging from "not passable" to "outstanding." As a matter of fact, it is possible to achieve a relatively low score without a single "incorrect" answer because of evident weakness in the qualities being measured.

Occasionally, an examination may consist entirely of an oral test – either an individual or a group oral. In such cases, information is sought concerning the technical knowledges and abilities of the candidate, since there has been no written examination for this purpose. More commonly, however, an oral test is used to supplement a written examination.

Who conducts interviews?

The composition of oral boards varies among different jurisdictions. In nearly all, a representative of the personnel department serves as chairman. One of the members of the board may be a representative of the department in which the candidate would work. In some cases, "outside experts" are used, and, frequently, a businessman or some other representative of the general public is asked to serve. Labor and management or other special groups may be represented. The aim is to secure the services of experts in the appropriate field.

However the board is composed, it is a good idea (and not at all improper or unethical) to ascertain in advance of the interview who the members are and what groups they represent. When you are introduced to them, you will have some idea of their backgrounds and interests, and at least you will not stutter and stammer over their names.

What should be done before the interview?

While knowledge about the board members is useful and takes some of the surprise element out of the interview, there is other preparation which is more substantive. It *is* possible to prepare for an oral interview – in several ways:

1) Keep a copy of your application and review it carefully before the interview

This may be the only document before the oral board, and the starting point of the interview. Know what education and experience you have listed there, and the sequence and dates of all of it. Sometimes the board will ask you to review the highlights of your experience for them; you should not have to hem and haw doing it.

2) Study the class specification and the examination announcement

Usually, the oral board has one or both of these to guide them. The qualities, characteristics or knowledges required by the position sought are stated in these documents. They offer valuable clues as to the nature of the oral interview. For example, if the job involves supervisory responsibilities, the announcement will usually indicate that knowledge of modern supervisory methods and the qualifications of the candidate as a supervisor will be tested. If so, you can expect such questions, frequently in the form of a hypothetical situation which you are expected to solve. NEVER go into an oral without knowledge of the duties and responsibilities of the job you seek.

3) Think through each qualification required

Try to visualize the kind of questions you would ask if you were a board member. How well could you answer them? Try especially to appraise your own knowledge and background in each area, *measured against the job sought*, and identify any areas in which you are weak. Be critical and realistic – do not flatter yourself.

4) Do some general reading in areas in which you feel you may be weak

For example, if the job involves supervision and your past experience has NOT, some general reading in supervisory methods and practices, particularly in the field of human relations, might be useful. Do NOT study agency procedures or detailed manuals. The oral board will be testing your understanding and capacity, not your memory.

5) Get a good night's sleep and watch your general health and mental attitude

You will want a clear head at the interview. Take care of a cold or any other minor ailment, and of course, no hangovers.

What should be done on the day of the interview?

Now comes the day of the interview itself. Give yourself plenty of time to get there. Plan to arrive somewhat ahead of the scheduled time, particularly if your appointment is in the fore part of the day. If a previous candidate fails to appear, the board might be ready for you a bit early. By early afternoon an oral board is almost invariably behind schedule if there are many candidates, and you may have to wait. Take along a book or magazine to read, or your application to review, but leave any extraneous material in the waiting room when you go in for your interview. In any event, relax and compose yourself.

The matter of dress is important. The board is forming impressions about you – from your experience, your manners, your attitude, and your appearance. Give your personal appearance careful attention. Dress your best, but not your flashiest. Choose conservative, appropriate clothing, and be sure it is immaculate. This is a business interview, and your appearance should indicate that you regard it as such. Besides, being well groomed and properly dressed will help boost your confidence.

Sooner or later, someone will call your name and escort you into the interview room. *This is it.* From here on you are on your own. It is too late for any more preparation. But remember, you asked for this opportunity to prove your fitness, and you are here because your request was granted.

What happens when you go in?

The usual sequence of events will be as follows: The clerk (who is often the board stenographer) will introduce you to the chairman of the oral board, who will introduce you to the other members of the board. Acknowledge the introductions before you sit down. Do not be surprised if you find a microphone facing you or a stenotypist sitting by. Oral interviews are usually recorded in the event of an appeal or other review.

Usually the chairman of the board will open the interview by reviewing the highlights of your education and work experience from your application – primarily for the benefit of the other members of the board, as well as to get the material into the record. Do not interrupt or comment unless there is an error or significant misinterpretation; if that is the case, do not hesitate. But do not quibble about insignificant matters. Also, he will usually ask you some question about your education, experience or your present job – partly to get you to start talking and to establish the interviewing "rapport." He may start the actual questioning, or turn it over to one of the other members. Frequently, each member undertakes the questioning on a particular area, one in which he is perhaps most competent, so you can expect each member to participate in the examination. Because time is limited, you may also expect some rather abrupt switches in the direction the questioning takes, so do not be upset by it. Normally, a board member will not pursue a single line of questioning unless he discovers a particular strength or weakness.

After each member has participated, the chairman will usually ask whether any member has any further questions, then will ask you if you have anything you wish to add. Unless you are expecting this question, it may floor you. Worse, it may start you off on an extended, extemporaneous speech. The board is not usually seeking more information. The question is principally to offer you a last opportunity to present further qualifications or to indicate that you have nothing to add. So, if you feel that a significant qualification or characteristic has been overlooked, it is proper to point it out in a sentence or so. Do not compliment the board on the thoroughness of their examination – they have been sketchy, and you know it. If you wish, merely say, "No thank you, I have nothing further to add." This is a point where you can "talk yourself out" of a good impression or fail to present an important bit of information. Remember, *you close the interview yourself.*

The chairman will then say, "That is all, Mr. _____, thank you." Do not be startled; the interview is over, and quicker than you think. Thank him, gather your belongings and take your leave. Save your sigh of relief for the other side of the door.

How to put your best foot forward

Throughout this entire process, you may feel that the board individually and collectively is trying to pierce your defenses, seek out your hidden weaknesses and embarrass and confuse you. Actually, this is not true. They are obliged to make an appraisal of your qualifications for the job you are seeking, and they want to see you in your best light. Remember, they must interview all candidates and a non-cooperative candidate may become a failure in spite of their best efforts to bring out his qualifications. Here are 15 suggestions that will help you:

1) Be natural – Keep your attitude confident, not cocky

If you are not confident that you can do the job, do not expect the board to be. Do not apologize for your weaknesses, try to bring out your strong points. The board is interested in a positive, not negative, presentation. Cockiness will antagonize any board member and make him wonder if you are covering up a weakness by a false show of strength.

2) Get comfortable, but don't lounge or sprawl

Sit erectly but not stiffly. A careless posture may lead the board to conclude that you are careless in other things, or at least that you are not impressed by the importance of the occasion. Either conclusion is natural, even if incorrect. Do not fuss with your clothing, a pencil or an ashtray. Your hands may occasionally be useful to emphasize a point; do not let them become a point of distraction.

3) Do not wisecrack or make small talk

This is a serious situation, and your attitude should show that you consider it as such. Further, the time of the board is limited – they do not want to waste it, and neither should you.

4) Do not exaggerate your experience or abilities

In the first place, from information in the application or other interviews and sources, the board may know more about you than you think. Secondly, you probably will not get away with it. An experienced board is rather adept at spotting such a situation, so do not take the chance.

5) If you know a board member, do not make a point of it, yet do not hide it

Certainly you are not fooling him, and probably not the other members of the board. Do not try to take advantage of your acquaintanceship – it will probably do you little good.

6) Do not dominate the interview

Let the board do that. They will give you the clues – do not assume that you have to do all the talking. Realize that the board has a number of questions to ask you, and do not try to take up all the interview time by showing off your extensive knowledge of the answer to the first one.

7) Be attentive

You only have 20 minutes or so, and you should keep your attention at its sharpest throughout. When a member is addressing a problem or question to you, give him your undivided attention. Address your reply principally to him, but do not exclude the other board members.

8) Do not interrupt

A board member may be stating a problem for you to analyze. He will ask you a question when the time comes. Let him state the problem, and wait for the question.

9) Make sure you understand the question

Do not try to answer until you are sure what the question is. If it is not clear, restate it in your own words or ask the board member to clarify it for you. However, do not haggle about minor elements.

10) Reply promptly but not hastily

A common entry on oral board rating sheets is "candidate responded readily," or "candidate hesitated in replies." Respond as promptly and quickly as you can, but do not jump to a hasty, ill-considered answer.

11) Do not be peremptory in your answers

A brief answer is proper – but do not fire your answer back. That is a losing game from your point of view. The board member can probably ask questions much faster than you can answer them.

12) Do not try to create the answer you think the board member wants

He is interested in what kind of mind you have and how it works – not in playing games. Furthermore, he can usually spot this practice and will actually grade you down on it.

13) Do not switch sides in your reply merely to agree with a board member

Frequently, a member will take a contrary position merely to draw you out and to see if you are willing and able to defend your point of view. Do not start a debate, yet do not surrender a good position. If a position is worth taking, it is worth defending.

14) Do not be afraid to admit an error in judgment if you are shown to be wrong

The board knows that you are forced to reply without any opportunity for careful consideration. Your answer may be demonstrably wrong. If so, admit it and get on with the interview.

15) Do not dwell at length on your present job

The opening question may relate to your present assignment. Answer the question but do not go into an extended discussion. You are being examined for a *new* job, not your present one. As a matter of fact, try to phrase ALL your answers in terms of the job for which you are being examined.

Basis of Rating

Probably you will forget most of these "do's" and "don'ts" when you walk into the oral interview room. Even remembering them all will not ensure you a passing grade. Perhaps you did not have the qualifications in the first place. But remembering them will help you to put your best foot forward, without treading on the toes of the board members.

Rumor and popular opinion to the contrary notwithstanding, an oral board wants you to make the best appearance possible. They know you are under pressure – but they also want to see how you respond to it as a guide to what your reaction would be under the pressures of the job you seek. They will be influenced by the degree of poise you display, the personal traits you show and the manner in which you respond.

ABOUT THIS BOOK

This book contains tests divided into Examination Sections. Go through each test, answering every question in the margin. We have also attached a sample answer sheet at the back of the book that can be removed and used. At the end of each test look at the answer key and check your answers. On the ones you got wrong, look at the right answer choice and learn. Do not fill in the answers first. Do not memorize the questions and answers, but understand the answer and principles involved. On your test, the questions will likely be different from the samples. Questions are changed and new ones added. If you understand these past questions you should have success with any changes that arise. Tests may consist of several types of questions. We have additional books on each subject should more study be advisable or necessary for you. Finally, the more you study, the better prepared you will be. This book is intended to be the last thing you study before you walk into the examination room. Prior study of relevant texts is also recommended. NLC publishes some of these in our Fundamental Series. Knowledge and good sense are important factors in passing your exam. Good luck also helps. So now study this Passbook, absorb the material contained within and take that knowledge into the examination. Then do your best to pass that exam.

EXAMINATION SECTION

EXAMINATION SECTION
TEST 1

DIRECTIONS: Each question or incomplete statement is followed by several suggested answers or completions. Select the one that BEST answers the question or completes the statement. *PRINT THE LETTER OF THE CORRECT ANSWER IN THE SPACE AT THE RIGHT.*

1. In filing records by subject, you should be MOST concerned with the   1._____

   A. name of the sender
   B. main topic of the letter
   C. date of the correspondence
   D. alphabetic cross reference

2. When arranging the medical record cards of patients in alphabetical order, the one of the following which should be filed THIRD is   2._____

   A. Charles A. Clarke   B. James Clark
   C. Joan Carney   D. Mae Cohen

3. The one of the following names which should be filed FIRST is   3._____

   A. Benjamin Dermody   B. Frank Davidson
   C. Matthew Davids   D. Seymour Diana

4. Vital statistics include data relating to   4._____

   A. births, deaths, and marriages
   B. the cost of food, clothing, and shelter
   C. the number of children per family unit
   D. diseases and their comparative mortality rates

Questions 5-10.

DIRECTIONS: Questions 5 through 10 are to be answered on the basis of the usual rules for alphabetical filing. For each question, indicate in the space at the right the letter preceding the name which should be filed THIRD in alphabetical order.

5. A. Hesselberg, Norman J.   B. Hesselman, Nathan B.   5._____
   C. Hazel, Robert S.   D. Heintz, August J.

6. A. Oshins, Jerome   B. O'Shaugn, F.J.   6._____
   C. O'Shaugn, F.J.   D. O'Shea, Frances

7. A. Petrie, Joshua A.   B. Pendleton, Oscar   7._____
   C. Pertwee, Joshua   D. Perkins, Warren G.

8. A. Morganstern, Alfred   B. Morganstern, Albert   8._____
   C. Monroe, Mildred   D. Modesti, Ernest

9. A. More, Stewart   B. Moorhead, Jay   9._____
   C. Moore, Benjamin   D. Moffat, Edith

10. A. Ramirez, Paul   B. Revere, Pauline   10.____
      C. Ramos, Felix   D. Ramazotti, Angelo

Questions 11-20.

DIRECTIONS: Questions 11 through 20 are to be answered on the basis of the usual rules of filing. Column I lists, next to the numbers 11 to 20, the names of 10 clinic patients. Column II lists, next to the letters A to D, the headings of file drawers into which you are to place the medical records of these patients. For each question, indicate in the space at the right the letter preceding the heading of the file drawer in which the record should be filed.

COLUMN I   COLUMN II

11. Charles Coughlin   A. Cab-Cep   11.____

12. Mary Carstairs   B. Ceq-Cho   12.____

13. Joseph Collin   C. Chr-Coj   13.____

14. Thomas Chelsey   D. Cok-Czy   14.____

15. Cedric Chalmers   15.____

16. Mae Clarke   16.____

17. Dora Copperhead   17.____

18. Arnold Cohn   18.____

19. Charlotte Crumboldt   19.____

20. Frances Celine   20.____

Questions 21-25.

DIRECTIONS: Questions 21 through 25 are to be answered on the basis of the chart below.

ATTENDANCE OF PATIENTS AT Y HEALTH CENTER
FOR WEEK OF APRIL 10

CLINIC	NUMBER SUMMONED FOR				NUMBER REPORTED TO			
	BABY	CHEST	EYE	V.D.	BABY	CHEST	EYE	V.D.
Monday	30	42	36	38	29	40	33	35
Tuesday	33	29	34	37	30	29	31	36
Wednesday	38	31	45	42	35	30	40	40
Thursday	41	48	41	32	36	45	39	28
Friday	35	37	39	36	33	35	37	32

21. On the basis of the above chart, it is CORRECT to say that _____ Clinic during the week.

    A. more patients were summoned to the Baby Clinic than to the Chest
    B. the same number of patients were absent from the Eye Clinic and the Baby
    C. more patients reported to the Eye Clinic than to the Chest
    D. more patients were summoned to the V.D. Clinic than to the Eye

22. On the basis of the above chart, the daily average number of patients summoned to the Eye Clinic exceeds the daily average reporting to the Eye Clinic by

    A. 3 B. 7 C. 11 D. 15

23. The percentage of all patients summoned to Y Health Center on Thursday who failed to report for their appointments is

    A. less than 5%
    B. more than 5% but less than 10%
    C. more than 10% but less than 15%
    D. more than 15%

24. The number of patients summoned for the entire week to the Eye Clinic exceeds the number of patients summoned to the Baby Clinic by

    A. 6 B. 9 C. 13 D. 18

25. The total number of patients who reported to Y Health Center for the week is

    A. 683 B. 693 C. 724 D. 744

KEY (CORRECT ANSWERS)

1. B
2. A
3. C
4. A
5. A

6. D
7. C
8. B
9. B
10. C

11. D
12. A
13. D
14. B
15. B

16. C
17. D
18. C
19. D
20. A

21. C
22. A
23. B
24. D
25. B

TEST 2

DIRECTIONS: Each question or incomplete statement is followed by several suggested answers or completions. Select the one that BEST answers the question or completes the statement. *PRINT THE LETTER OF THE CORRECT ANSWER IN THE SPACE AT THE RIGHT.*

Questions 1-8.

DIRECTIONS: Questions 1 through 8 are to be answered on the basis of the usual rules of filing. Column I lists, next to the numbers 1 to 8, the names of 8 clinic patients. Column II lists, next to the letters A to O, the headings of file drawers into which you are to place the records of these patients. In the space at the right, corresponding to each name listed in Column I, print the letter preceding the heading of the file drawer in which the record should be filed.

COLUMN I		COLUMN II	
1.	Thomas Adams	A.	Aab-Abi
2.	Joseph Albert	B.	Abj-Ach
3.	Frank Anaster	C.	Aci-Aco
4.	Charles Abt	D.	Acp-Ada
5.	John Alfred	E.	Adb-Afr
6.	Louis Aron	F.	Afs-Ago
7.	Francis Amos	G.	Agp-Ahz
8.	William Adler	H.	Aia-Ako
		I.	Akp-Ald
		J.	Ale-Amo
		K.	Amp-Aor
		L.	Aos-Apr
		M.	Aps-Asi
		N.	Asj-Ati
		O.	Atj-Awz

1.___
2.___
3.___
4.___
5.___
6.___
7.___
8.___

Questions 9-14.

DIRECTIONS: In answering Questions 9 through 14, alphabetize the four names listed in each question; then print in the corresponding space at the right the letter of the answer containing the four numbers preceding the alphabetized names to show the CORRECT alphabetical arrangement of the four names.

9. 1. Frank Adam   2. Frank Aarons
    3. Frank Aaron   4. Frank Adams
    The CORRECT answer is:

    A. 2, 3, 1, 4   B. 4, 2, 1, 3
    C. 1, 2, 4, 3   D. 3, 2, 1, 4

10. 1. Richard Lavine   2. Richard Levine
    3. Edward Lawrence   4. Edward Loraine
    The CORRECT answer is:

    A. 1, 2, 3, 4   B. 3, 1, 2, 4
    C. 1, 3, 2, 4   D. 2, 4, 3, 1

11. 1. G. Frank Adam   2. Frank Adam
    3. Fanny Adam   4. Franklin Adam
    The CORRECT answer is:

    A. 3, 4, 1, 2   B. 2, 1, 3, 4
    C. 3, 2, 4, 1   D. 2, 3, 4, 1

12. 1. George Cohn   2. Richard Cohen
    3. Thomas Cohane   4. George Cohan
    The CORRECT answer is:

    A. 2, 1, 3, 4   B. 4, 1, 3, 2
    C. 3, 1, 4, 2   D. 4, 3, 2, 1

13. 1. Paul Shultz   2. Robert Schmid
    3. Joseph Schwartz   4. Edward Schmidt
    The CORRECT answer is:

    A. 2, 4, 3, 1   B. 2, 1, 3, 4
    C. 3, 4, 1, 2   D. 1, 2, 4, 3

14. 1. Peter Consilazio   2. Frank Consolezio
    3. Robert Consalizio   4. Ella Consolizio
    The CORRECT answer is:

    A. 3, 4, 1, 2   B. 3, 1, 2, 4
    C. 1, 2, 4, 3   D. 3, 2, 1, 4

Questions 15-25.

DIRECTIONS: For Questions 15 through 25, select the letter preceding the word which means MOST NEARLY the same as the word in capitals.

15. LEGIBLE

    A. readable   B. eligible   C. learned   D. lawful

16. OBSERVE

    A. assist   B. watch   C. correct   D. oppose

17. HABITUAL

    A. punctual   B. occasional
    C. usual   D. actual

18. CHRONOLOGICAL   18.____
    A. successive   B. earlier
    C. later   D. studious

19. ARREST   19.____
    A. punish   B. run   C. threaten   D. stop

20. ABSTAIN   20.____
    A. refrain   B. indulge   C. discolor   D. spoil

21. TOXIC   21.____
    A. poisonous   B. decaying
    C. taxing   D. defective

22. TOLERATE   22.____
    A. fear   B. forgive   C. allow   D. despise

23. VENTILATE   23.____
    A. vacate   B. air   C. extricate   D. heat

24. SUPERIOR   24.____
    A. perfect   B. subordinate
    C. lower   D. higher

25. EXTREMITY   25.____
    A. extent   B. limb   C. illness   D. execution

KEY (CORRECT ANSWERS)

1. D   11. C
2. I   12. D
3. K   13. A
4. B   14. B
5. J   15. A

6. M   16. B
7. J   17. C
8. E   18. A
9. D   19. D
10. C   20. A

21. A
22. C
23. B
24. D
25. B

TEST 3

DIRECTIONS: Each question or incomplete statement is followed by several suggested answers or completions. Select the one that BEST answers the question or completes the statement. *PRINT THE LETTER OF THE CORRECT ANSWER IN THE SPACE AT THE RIGHT.*

Questions 1-20.

DIRECTIONS: Column I below lists words used in medical practice. Column II lists phrases which describe the words in Column I. In the space at the right, opposite the number preceding each of the words in Column I, place the letter preceding the phrase in Column II which BEST describes the word in Column I.

COLUMN I

1. Abrasion
2. Aseptic
3. Cardiac
4. Catarrh
5. Contamination
6. Dermatology
7. Disinfectant
8. Dyspepsia
9. Epidemic
10. Epidermis
11. Incubation
12. Microscope
13. Pediatrics
14. Plasma
15. Prenatal
16. Retina
17. Syphilis
18. Syringe
19. Toxemia
20. Vaccine

COLUMN II

A. A disturbance of digestion
B. Destroying the germs of disease
C. A general poisoning of the blood
D. An instrument used for injecting fluids
E. A scraping off of the skin
F. Free from disease germs
G. An apparatus for viewing internal organs by means of x-rays
H. An instrument for assisting the eye in observing minute objects
I. An inoculable immunizing agent
J. The extensive prevalence in a community of a disease
K. Chemical product of an organ
L. Preceding birth
M. Fever
N. Branch of medical science that relates to skin and its diseases
O. Fluid part of the blood
P. The science of hygienic care of children
Q. Infection by contact
R. Relating to the heart
S. Inner structure of the eye
T. Outer portion of the skin
U. Pertaining to the ductless glands
V. An infectious venereal disease
X. The development of an infectious disease from the period of infection to that of the appearance of the first symptoms
Y. Simple inflammation of a mucous membrane
Z. An instrument for measuring blood pressure

1. ____
2. ____
3. ____
4. ____
5. ____
6. ____
7. ____
8. ____
9. ____
10. ____
11. ____
12. ____
13. ____
14. ____
15. ____
16. ____
17. ____
18. ____
19. ____
20. ____

21. The fluoroscope is used CHIEFLY to 21.___
    A. provide a permanent picture of the condition of internal organs at a given time
    B. make a chart of the action of the muscles of the heart
    C. observe the internal structure and functioning of the organs of the body at a given time
    D. produce heat in the tissues of the body

22. A stethoscope is an instrument used for 22.___
    A. determining the blood pressure
    B. taking the body temperature
    C. chest examinations
    D. determining the amount of sugar in the blood

23. The Dick test is used to determine susceptibility to 23.___
    A. measles   B. scarlet fever
    C. diphtheria   D. chicken pox

24. The aorta is a(n) 24.___
    A. bone   B. artery   C. ligament   D. nerve

25. The esophagus is part of the 25.___
    A. alimentary canal   B. abdominal wall
    C. mucous membrane   D. circulatory system

KEY (CORRECT ANSWERS)

1.	E	11.	X
2.	F	12.	H
3.	R	13.	P
4.	Y	14.	O
5.	Q	15.	L
6.	N	16.	S
7.	B	17.	V
8.	A	18.	D
9.	J	19.	C
10.	T	20.	I

21. C
22. C
23. B
24. B
25. A

EXAMINATION SECTION
TEST 1

DIRECTIONS: Each question or incomplete statement is followed by several suggested answers or completions. Select the one that BEST answers the question or completes the statement. *PRINT THE LETTER OF THE CORRECT ANSWER IN THE SPACE AT THE RIGHT.*

1. According to one suggested filing system, no more than 12 folders should be filed behind any one file guide and from 10 to 20 file guides should be used in each file drawer. Based on this filing system, the MAXIMUM number of folders that a four-drawer file cabinet can hold is

    A. 240 B. 480 C. 960 D. 1200

2. A certain office uses three different forms. Last year it used 3500 copies of Form L, 6700 copies of Form M, and 10,500 copies of Form P. This year, the office expects to decrease the use of each of these forms by 5%.
The TOTAL number of these three forms which the office expects to use this year is

    A. 10,350 B. 16,560 C. 19,665 D. 21,735

3. The hourly rate of pay for a certain part-time employee is computed by dividing his yearly salary rate by the number of hours in the work year. The employee's yearly salary rate is $18,928, and there are 1,820 hours in the work year.
If this employee works 18 hours during one week, his TOTAL earnings for these 18 hours are

    A. $180.00 B. $183.60 C. $187.20 D. $190.80

4. Assume that the regular work week of an employee is 35 hours and that the employee is paid for any extra hours worked according to the following schedule. For hours worked in excess of 35 hours, up to and including 40 hours, the employee receives his regular hourly rate of pay. For hours worked in excess of 40 hours, the employee receives 1 1/2 times his hourly rate of pay.
If the employee's hourly rate of pay is $11.20 and he works 43 hours during a certain week, his TOTAL pay for the week would be

    A. $481.60 B. $498.40 C. $556.00 D. $722.40

5. The following table shows the total amount of money owed on the bills sent to each of four different accounts and the total amount of money which has been received from each of these accounts.

Name of Account	Amount Owed	Amount Received
Arnold	$55,989	$37,898
Barry	$97,276	$79,457
Carter	$62,736	$47,769
Daley	$77,463	$59,534

    The balance of an account is determined by subtracting the amount received from the amount owed. Based on this method of determining a balance, the account with the LARGEST balance is

    A. Arnold B. Barry C. Carter D. Daley

6. Suppose that you are transferring the charges of a number of hospital patients from each patient's individual records to one form.
To make sure that the amounts are transferred accurately, it would be BEST for you to

   A. check each amount copies against the appropriate patient's records after completing the transfers
   B. have someone read the amounts from the patient records while you write them on the form
   C. copy the amounts slowly and carefully so that you will not make a mistake
   D. write each amount lightly in pencil and then go over each number heavily with a pen

6.____

7. Assume that your office ordered supplies from a vendor on December 1. These supplies are to be used starting on February 2 of the following year, and it is essential that they arrive by that date.
Of the following, which is the BEST way to assure that the supplies arrive on time?

   A. Contact the post office before February 2 and inquire about the vendor's record in shipping supplies
   B. Keep in contact with the vendor until the supplies arrive, and follow up on any problems which arise
   C. Mail a duplicate copy of the order to the vendor sometime in January to serve as a reminder
   D. Telephone the vendor a week before February 2, and ask whether the supplies were shipped

7.____

8. Assume that you are working in an admissions area of a hospital and you are completing an admissions form for a new patient. In order to complete the form, you have to obtain certain information from the patient, such as his name, address, and age, and write it on the form.
Of the following, the FIRST action you should take after the patient tells you his name is to

   A. ask the patient for a copy of his birth certificate in order to verify his name
   B. ask the patient whether he has been a patient in your hospital before
   C. tell the patient to write his name on the form
   D. write his name in the appropriate place on the admissions form

8.____

9. Of the following, the BEST reason for a clerical division to have its own photocopying machine is that the division

   A. frequently needs copies of incoming correspondence
   B. frequently receives photographic negatives in the mail
   C. must enter the receipt date on all incoming mail
   D. uses 5,000 copies of a form each month

9.____

10. In your assignment to a hospital admitting office, you will be required to personally fill out an admissions form for each person before he is admitted to the hospital. Of the following, the MOST accurate way for you to obtain the information you need from a person is to

    A. ask him one question at a time based on the information you need
    B. ask him only those questions which can be answered by the words *yes* or *no*

10.____

C. give him the form and tell him to fill it out correctly
D. have him complete the entire form and then sign it yourself

Questions 11-20.

DIRECTIONS: Each of Questions 11 through 20 gives the identification number and name of aperson who has received treatment at a certain hospital. You are to choose the option (A, B, C, or D) which has EXACTLY the same identification number and name as those given in the question.

SAMPLE QUESTION

123765 Frank Y. Jones

A. 123675 Frank Y. Jones
B. 123765 Frank T. Jones
C. 123765 Frank Y. Johns
D. 123765 Frank Y. Jones

The correct answer is D. Only option D shows the identification number and name exactly as they are in the sample question. Option A has a mistake in the identification number. Option B has a mistake in the middle initial of the name. Option C has a mistake in the last name.

Now answer Questions 11 through 20 in the same manner.

11. 754898 Diane Malloy

 A. 745898   Diane Malloy
 B. 754898   Dion Malloy
 C. 754898   Diane Malloy
 D. 754898   Diane Maloy

12. 661018 Ferdinand Figueroa

 A. 661818   Ferdinand Figeuroa
 B. 661618   Ferdinand Figueroa
 C. 661818   Ferdnand Figueroa
 D. 661818   Ferdinand Figueroa

13. 100101 Norman D. Braustein

 A. 100101   Norman D. Braustein
 B. 101001   Norman D. Braustein
 C. 100101   Norman P. Braustien
 D. 100101   Norman D. Bruastein

14. 838696 Robert Kittredge

 A. 838969   Robert Kittredge
 B. 838696   Robert Kittredge
 C. 388696   Robert Kittredge
 D. 838696   Robert Kittridge

4 (#1)

15. 243716   Abraham Soletsky   15.____

    A. 243716   Abrahm Soletsky
    B. 243716   Abraham Solestky
    C. 243176   Abraham Soletsky
    D. 243716   Abraham Soletsky

16. 981121   Phillip M. Maas   16.____

    A. 981121   Phillip M. Mass
    B. 981211   Phillip M. Maas
    C. 981121   Phillip M. Maas
    D. 981121   Phillip N. Maas

17. 786556   George Macalusso   17.____

    A. 785656   George Macalusso
    B. 786556   George Macalusso
    C. 786556   George Maculasso
    D. 786556   George Macluasso

18. 639472   Eugene Weber   18.____

    A. 639472   Eugene Weber
    B. 639472   Eugene Webre
    C. 693472   Eugene Weber
    D. 639742   Eugene Weber

19. 724936   John J. Lomonaco   19.____

    A. 724936   John J. Lomanoco
    B. 724396   John J. Lomonaco
    C. 724936   John J. Lomonaco
    D. 724936   John J. Lamonaco

20. 899868   Michael Schnitzer   20.____

    A. 899868   Micheal Schnitzer
    B. 898968   Michael Schnizter
    C. 899688   Michael Schnitzer
    D. 899868   Michael Schnitzer

KEY (CORRECT ANSWERS)

1. C
2. C
3. C
4. B
5. A
6. A
7. A
8. D
9. A
10. A

11. C
12. D
13. A
14. B
15. D
16. C
17. B
18. A
19. C
20. D

———

TEST 2

DIRECTIONS: Each question or incomplete statement is followed by several suggested answers or completions. Select the one that BEST answers the question or completes the statement. *PRINT THE LETTER OF TEE CORRECT ANSWER IN THE SPACE AT THE RIGHT.*

Questions 1-10.

DIRECTIONS: Questions 1 through 10 are to be answered on the basis of the information and the form given below.

The form below is a Daily Summary of Clinic Visits and lists ten persons who used a clinic in Washington Hospital on September 4.

The form includes the following information about each patient: Name, identification number, date of birth, case number, fee, and bill number.

SEPTEMBER 4 WASHINGTON HOSPITAL - DAILY SUMMARY OF CLINIC VISITS							
Name of Patient Last, First	Identification Number	Date of Birth			Case Number	Fee	Bill Number
			Mo.	Day	Yr.			
Enders, John	89-4143-67	08	01	71	434317	$ 90.00	129631
Dawes, Mary	71-6142-69	11	17	66	187963	$ 47.50	129632
Lang, Donald	54-1213-73	10	07	75	897436	$180.00	129633
Eiger, Alan	18-7649-63	06	19	51	134003	$110.00	129634
Ramirez, Jose	61-4319-69	03	30	96	379030	$130.00	129635
Ilono, Frank	13-9161-57	08	19	83	565645	$ 66.00	129636
Sloan, Irene	55-8643-66	05	13	57	799732	$112.50	129637
Long, Thomas	41-3963-74	12	03	76	009784	$ 37.50	129638
McKay, Cathy	14-9633-44	05	09	66	000162	$ 96.00	129639
Dale, Sarah	86-1113-69	11	13	59	543211	$138.00	129640

1. The fee for Cathy McKay is LESS than the fee for 1.____

   A. John Enders B. Alan Eiger
   C. Frank Ilono D. Thomas Long

2. The two patients who were born in the same year are 2.____

   A. John Enders and Frank Ilono
   B. Mary Dawes and Sarah Dale
   C. Donald Lang and Thomas Long
   D. Cathy McKay and Mary Dawes

3. The case number of Irene Sloan is 3.____

   A. 979732   B. 799372   C. 799732   D. 797732

4. Cathy McKay's identification number is 4.____

   A. 44-9633-14   B. 14-9633-44
   C. 000162   D. 129639

14

5. Frank Ilono's case number is 5._____

    A. 556645   B. 565465   C. 565645   D. 565654

6. The bill numbers for Jose Ramirez and Thomas Long are 6._____

    A. 129635 and 129638   B. 129635 and 129683
    C. 129634 and 129638   D. 129634 and 129637

7. The fees for Donald Lang, Sarah Dale, and Mary Dawes are 7._____

    A. $47.50, $180.00, and $96.00
    B. $110.00, $138.00, and $90.00
    C. $180.00, $130.00, and $47.50
    D. $180.00, $138.00, and $47.50

8. The case numbers for Thomas Long and Mary Dawes are 8._____

    A. 009784 and 187963   B. 090784 and 187963
    C. 009784 and 187693   D. 009874 and 187963

9. The identification numbers for Frank Ilono and Donald Lang are 9._____

    A. 13-9161-57 and 54-1312-73
    B. 54-1213-73 and 13-6191-57
    C. 13-9161-57 and 54-1213-73
    D. 54-1213-37 and 13-9161-57

10. The birth dates of Irene Sloan, John Enders, and Sarah Dale are 10._____

    A. 05/31/57, 01/08/71, and 11/13/69
    B. 05/13/67, 08/01/71, and 11/13/69
    C. 05/31/57, 01/08/71, and 11/13/59
    D. 05/13/57, 08/01/71, and 11/13/59

Questions 11-15.

DIRECTIONS: Questions 11 through 15 consist of sets of names and addresses. In each question, the name and address in Column II should be an EXACT copy of the name and address in Column I. Compare the name and address in Column II with the name and address in Column I.

    If there is an error in the name only, mark your answer A;
    If there is an error in the address only, mark your answer B;
    If there is an error in both the name and address, mark your answer C;
    If there is NO error in either the name or address, mark your answer D.

SAMPLE QUESTION

COLUMN I	COLUMN II
Mildred Bonilla	Mildred Bonila
511 West 186 Street	511 West 186 Street
New York, N.Y. 10033	New York, N.Y. 10032

Compare the name and address in Column II with the name and address in Column I. The name <u>Bonila</u> in Column II is spelled <u>Bonilla</u> in Column I. The zip code <u>10032</u> in Column II is given as <u>10033</u> in Column I. Since there is an error in both the name and address, the answer to the sample question is C.

Now answer Questions 11 through 15 in the same manner.

<u>COLUMN I</u>   <u>COLUMN II</u>

11. Mr. & Mrs. George Petersson   Mr. & Mrs. George Peterson   11.____
    87-11 91st Avenue   87-11 91st Avenue
    Woodhaven, New York 11421   Woodhaven, New York 11421

12. Mr. Ivan Klebnikov   Mr. Ivan Klebikov   12.____
    1848 Newkirk Avenue   1848 Newkirk Avenue
    Brooklyn, New York 11226   Brooklyn, New York 11622

13. Samuel Rothfleisch   Samuel Rothfleisch   13.____
    71 Pine Street   71 Pine Street
    New York, New York 10005   New York, New York 10005

14. Mrs. Isabel Tonnessen   Mrs. Isabel Tonnessen   14.____
    198 East 185th Street   189 East 185th Street
    Bronx, New York 10458   Bronx, New York 10458

15. Esteban Perez   Estaban Perez   15.____
    173 Eighth Street   173 Eighth Street
    Staten Island, N.Y. 10306   Staten Island, N.Y. 10306

16. The MAIN purpose of an invoice is to   16.____

    A. confirm receipt of an order
    B. list items being sent to a buyer
    C. order items from a company
    D. provide written proof that a shipment has been received

17. You have been told to add various amounts listed on a billing form by operating a calcu-   17.____
    lating machine. The machine prints on a roll of paper tape all amounts added and the
    answer to the computation.
    Of the following, the LEAST appropriate use for this tape is to

    A. check that no amounts were left out during the computation
    B. check that the amounts were entered correctly into the machine
    C. keep a record of the computation
    D. prove that the amounts on the original document are correct

18. Assume that you are working in a storehouse of a hospital system. One of your tasks is   18.____
    to fill requisitions from hospitals for office supplies. When a requisition is received, you
    much check inventory cards to determine whether an item is available. One day, you
    receive a requisition for office supplies; and upon checking the inventory cards, you find
    that one of the items ordered, a particular kind of paper, is not available. However, the
    other items are ready for shipment to the hospital. Of the following, the BEST course of
    action for you to take in this situation is to

A. have those items which are available sent to the hospital with an indication of which items were sent
B. purchase the missing paper yourself and then have the complete order sent to the hospital
C. substitute any other paper which is available and then have the order sent to the hospital
D. wait until the missing paper is available and then have the complete order sent to the hospital

19. One of your duties is to get certain information from people who are being treated at a hospital clinic. One day, you are trying to get this information from a person who begins to talk about matters unrelated to the information you are trying to obtain.
Of the following, the BEST course of action for you to take in this situation is to

    A. allow the individual to continue talking about the unrelated matters since he will probably return to the information you need in a short time
    B. ask the individual a question that may lead him back to the information you need
    C. end the interview and obtain the information from other sources
    D. tell the individual to give you the information you need and not discuss the unrelated matters

19._____

20. You have just asked a patient a question about the kind of hospitalization insurance he has.
The BEST way for you to make sure that you understand his answer to the question is to

    A. ask the question again in a slightly different way and see if you get approximately the same answer
    B. ask the same question again and listen carefully to see if the answer is the same
    C. repeat the answer in your own words and ask the patient if that is what he meant
    D. write the answer down on a piece of paper and read it back to the patient

20._____

KEY (CORRECT ANSWERS)

1.	B	11.	A
2.	D	12.	C
3.	C	13.	D
4.	B	14.	B
5.	C	15.	A
6.	A	16.	B
7.	D	17.	D
8.	A	18.	A
9.	C	19.	B
10.	D	20.	C

EXAMINATION SECTION
TEST 1

DIRECTIONS: Each question or incomplete statement is followed by several suggested answers or completions. Select the one that BEST answers the question or completes the statement. *PRINT THE LETTER OF THE CORRECT ANSWER IN THE SPACE AT THE RIGHT.*

1. According to the Joint Commission on the Accreditation of Health Care Organizations, medical records must meet _____ standard(s) of performance. 1.____

    A. one   B. two   C. four   D. five

2. The MAIN purpose of medical records is to provide a vehicle for 2.____

    A. documenting action taken in patient management
    B. documenting patient progress
    C. providing meaningful medical information to other practitioners
    D. all of the above

3. According to the JCAHO manual, all of the following information must be included in all medical records EXCEPT 3.____

    A. medical history of the patient
    B. events occurring after discharge from the hospital
    C. reports of relevant physical examination
    D. reports of procedures, tests, and their results

4. Medical records of the licensed and certified health care professional MUST contain 4.____

    A. dates of treatment
    B. action taken by non-licensed persons when ordered or authorized by the provider
    C. doctors' orders, nurses' notes and charts, birth certificate worksheets
    D. all of the above

5. According to the JCAHO manual, medical records must be completed within a period of time that does NOT exceed _____ days. 5.____

    A. 10   B. 20   C. 30   D. 40

6. Of the following, the CORRECT statement regarding medical record correction is: 6.____

    A. Errors should be erased or obliterated
    B. Errors should not be lined out
    C. Corrections should be initialed and dated
    D. All of the above

7. Individual health care providers MUST maintain patient records for _____ year(s) from the last date of treatment. 7.____

    A. one   B. three   C. five   D. seven

8. After the patient's death, an individual health care provider must maintain his record for _____ year(s).

   A. one B. three C. five D. seven

9. All of the following are true statements regarding health care providers EXCEPT:

   A. If a health care facility or organization retains medical records for a patient, the provider must maintain a duplicate set
   B. A health care provider must give public and private notice of his retirement to his patients
   C. Pathology slides and EEG and ECG tracings must be kept for seven years
   D. If a claim of malpractice or neglect of a patient is made, all records for that patient must be retained until the matter is resolved

10. To prevent the disclosure of medical records that must be destroyed, each provider should adopt a policy outlining destruction procedures, which should include

    A. the title of the person who may authorize destruction
    B. the data bases that would be affected
    C. the method of shipment of the records
    D. all of the above

11. Of the following, the confidentiality obligation in medical records is based on _____ factors.

    A. ethical B. legal
    C. therapeutic argument D. all of the above

12. Certified independent social workers may not disclose communication or records related to evaluation or treatment EXCEPT

    A. to other individuals engaged in diagnosis or treatment
    B. when there is a substantial risk of imminent injury to the person or others
    C. in an evaluation ordered by the court if the person concerned is informed in advance
    D. all of the above

13. All of the following individuals may act as the patient representative who reviews and receives copies of the patient's medical records EXCEPT a

    A. surrogate parent B. divorced parent
    C. brother D. patient's attorney

14. Consequences of wrongful disclosure may include

    A. invasion of privacy claim
    B. breach of duty of confidentiality
    C. breach of contract
    D. all of the above

15. When considering a request for disclosure subsequent to receiving the patient's consent, the provider should consider whether the

    A. authorization is specifically addressed to the institution
    B. authorization is signed by the patient

C. authorization is witnessed or notarized
D. all of the above

16. Of the following, the TRUE statement regarding incident reports is: 16.____

    A. Reports should be treated as confidential documents
    B. Incident report is not a part of medical records
    C. It is not necessary to address the reports to the institution's attorney
    D. All of the above

17. In medical terminology, the healing arts include the practice of 17.____

    A. medicine B. osteopathy
    C. chiropractice D. all of the above

18. Of the following, medical records contain _____ data about an individual patient. 18.____

    A. medical B. financial
    C. personal D. all of the above

19. A physician's verbal orders should be limited as much as possible to telephone orders and in all cases must be transcribed in the medical records and signed by the physician within 19.____

    A. 24 hours B. one week
    C. one month D. one year

20. Every time a patient visits the emergency department, all of the following information must be entered in the patient's medical record EXCEPT 20.____

    A. pertinent history of the illness or injury
    B. emergency care given to the patient prior to the arrival
    C. annual income
    D. patient identification

KEY (CORRECT ANSWERS)

1.	C	11.	D
2.	D	12.	D
3.	B	13.	C
4.	D	14.	D
5.	C	15.	D
6.	C	16.	A
7.	D	17.	D
8.	B	18.	D
9.	A	19.	A
10.	D	20.	C

EXAMINATION SECTION
TEST 1

DIRECTIONS: Each question or incomplete statement is followed by several suggested answers or completions. Select the one that BEST answers the question or completes the statement. *PRINT THE LETTER OF THE CORRECT ANSWER IN THE SPACE AT THE RIGHT.*

Medical Terminology

1. The term "papilloma" denotes a tumor that appears

    A. on a gland
    B. darkly pigmented
    C. as a small elevation
    D. in a scaly form

2. What is the term used to describe blood that is detectable by chemical test in stool or urine specimens?

    A. Meconium
    B. Precipitate
    C. Occult
    D. Residual

3. The mediastinum is

    A. the collapse of a lung with escape of air into the cavity between the lung and the chest wall
    B. the space in the middle of the chest between the lungs
    C. a malignant tumor occurring in the pleura, peritoneum or pericardium
    D. the membranous lining of the upper body cavity and covering for the lungs

4. Which of the following medical terms is used to denote a calculus in the pancreas?

    A. pancreatorrhaphy
    B. pancreatolith
    C. pancreatotomy
    D. pancreatopathy

5. Deficits in phosphorus and calcium sometimes cause a softening of the bone tissue, known as

    A. dysorthosis
    B. osteomalacia
    C. chondrostasis
    D. osteoporosis

6. In medical terms, which of the following is a suffix that means "pain"?

    A. -algia
    B. -osis
    C. -itis
    D. -taxia

7. The medical term describing an abnormally low amount of urine is

   A. polyuria
   B. oliguria
   C. uripenia
   D. anuria

8. In medical terms, the word "cephalocaudal" is a directional adjective describing a view or line that is directed

   A. side to middle
   B. front to back
   C. back and above
   D. head to tail

9. The medical term describing unequal pupil size is

   A. anisocoria
   B. strabismus
   C. corectasia
   D. ptosis

ICD-9-CM

10. Which of the following V codes should NEVER be used as a principal diagnosis?

    A. V24
    B. V29
    C. V62
    D. V58.5

11. An elderly woman is admitted to the emergency room after slipping on ice on her front porch and falling down several stairs. She landing hard on her right hip, and the fall resulted in right femoral neck fracture. What diagnosis codes should be reported?

    A. 820.9, E882.
    B. 821.3, E8880
    C. 820.8, E880.9
    D. 821.00

12. A child is brought to the emergency room in a coma after ingesting his mother's Thorazine. The correct diagnostic code for this case is

    A. 780.01, 969.1, E980.3
    B. 969.1, E980.3, 780.01
    C. 969.1, E853.0, 780.01
    D. 780.01, 969.1, E853.0

13. A patient suffered an acute CVA with infarction with left-sided hemiplegia, aphasia, and dysphagia. The hemiplegia and dysphagia cleared before discharge; only aphasia was present at discharge to rehabilitation. The appropriate diagnostic coding is

A. 434.91, 784.3
B. 434.91, 342.90, 787.2
C. 434.91, 342.90
D. 434.91, 342.90, 784.3, 787.2

14. Code for Alzheimer's dementia with behavioral disturbance: 14.____

    A. 331.0
    B. 331.0, 294.10
    C. 331.0, 294.11
    D. 331.2, 294.10

15. A patient's systolic blood pressure is over 160, but the patient has no history of hypertension, and the physician is reluctant to make this diagnosis based on a single visit. The diagnostic code for this visit would be 15.____

    A. 401.1
    B. 401.9
    C. 642.30
    D. 796.2

16. A patient is admitted with multiple burns. The FIRST code listed should be the one that reflects the 16.____

    A. highest degree of burn
    B. greatest single surface area of the body that has been burned
    C. exact number of burns
    D. least serious burn

17. Chapter 11 codes should be used unless pregnancy is incidental to the encounter, in which instance code _____ should be used in place of any Chapter 11 codes. 17.____

    A. 650
    B. V22.0
    C. V22.2
    D. E849.9

Payment Methodologies

18. A provider who accepts "assignment" for a Medicare patient 18.____

    A. is required to charge half or less of his/her customary fee
    B. is required to collect the patient's copayment up front
    C. agrees to collect the payment directly from the patient
    D. agrees to have Medicare pay him/her directly

19. A physician who expects a patient to remain in the hospital for more than 24 hours should 19.____

    A. keep the patient in observation for eight hours and admit the patient after that time period
    B. admit the patient for the time limit of observation
    C. admit the patient as an inpatient
    D. admit the patient to observation

20. Which of the following would be NOT included in the facility fee charge?

    A. Ambulance services
    B. Nursing services
    C. Housekeeping services
    D. Anesthesia materials

21. On CMS 1500, the number in box 24e should correspond to the one diagnosis code in box 21 that supports the procedure. This refers to

    A. revenue codes
    B. a crossover claim
    C. an EOB
    D. the linkage of ICD-9-CM and CPT codes

22. What is a "grouper?"

    A. Software that translates variables into DRGs
    B. Software used by Medicare hospitals to process outpatient claims
    C. A measure of the difference in resources among physician fee schedule areas
    D. Software that tracks the flow of a claim through the hospital and the different departments.

23. FL 16 of CMS 1450 is coded "X." This means that the patient

    A. is legally separated
    B. is divorced
    C. has no dependents
    D. died in the hospital

24. A procedure code with the status modifier _____ denotes a procedure that is NOT paid under Medicare OPPS.

    A. E   B. G   C. K   D. X

25. If a patient is injured while at work, one of the form locators (FLs) from 24-30 on CMS 1450 should be coded

    A. 01   B. 02   C. 03   D. 05

General CPT

26. The "surgical package" for major surgery contains a minimum _____ day postoperative period that includes all visits to the physician during that time unless the visit is for a totally different reason than that for the surgery.

    A. 30   B. 60   C. 90   D. 120

27. Code an extended second-opinion consult required by an HMO.　　27._____

    A. 99271
    B. 99205-99
    C. 99274-32
    D. 99275-23

28. Modifier 76 is used to indicate a(n)　　28._____

    A. unrelated procedure or service by the same physician during the postoperative period of the original surgery
    B. repeat procedure on the same day by another physician
    C. return trip to the operating room for a related procedure during the postoperative period of the original surgery
    D. repeat procedure on the same day by the same physician

29. 36 days after a patient had a lesion removed from her breast, the entire breast was removed in a modified radical mastectomy that included the axillary lymph nodes and the pectoralis minor muscle, but excluded the pectoralis major muscle. The correct code for this second procedure would be　　29._____

    A. 19120, 19240
    B. 19220-58
    C. 19240-58
    D. 19240

30. Code a limited study for transthoracic echocardiogram for congenital cardiac anomalies.　　30._____

    A. 93304x2
    B. 93304-26
    C. 93303
    D. 93304

31. In the CPT manual, a coder comes across an entry that is preceded by the symbol _. This means that　　31._____

    A. conscious sedation is included in the procedure
    B. is linked to a CPT Assistant article
    C. the code is exempt from the use of modifier 51
    D. it is a Level III code

32. A plus sign (+) that appears before a code in the CPT manual indicates that the code　　32._____

    A. is an add-on code that cannot be used alone
    B. indicates a new procedure that has been added since the most recent edition of the CPT manual
    C. involves special instructions
    D. is modifier 51 exempt

33. "Information Only" modifiers–which do not impact reimbursement–include each of the following, EXCEPT　　33._____

    A. 22　　　B. 24　　　C. 32　　　D. 57

34. Code for a laparoscopic fimbrioplasty.

    A. 58672
    B. 58673
    C. 58750
    D. 58760

35. A patient with attention deficit/hyperactivity disorder (ADDH) visits an outpatient hospital and receives 25 minutes of individual psychotherapy that was insight-oriented and aimed at modifying behavior. The most appropriate code for this visit is

    A. 90816, 314.1
    B. 90806, 314.01
    C. 90804, 314.00
    D. 90804, 314.01

Surgical Procedures

36. Code for the amputation of the left leg through the tibia and fibula.

    A. 27759
    B. 27880
    C. 27881
    D. 27882

37. A 74-year-old woman with gastric cancer and a subcutaneous port presents with a poorly functioning port. Infusion and injections can be made, but blood cannot be aspirated. A vascular snare is placed in the vein through the catheter, and the tip of the central venous catheter is engaged with the snare. The fibrin sheath and thrombus are stripped from the catheter.

    The appropriate CPT code for the procedure is

    A. 36861
    B. 36536
    C. 35476
    D. 36870

38. A patient reports to the emergency room with a torn fingernail and a subungual hematoma on his nail bed. After the patient's right hand was soaked in Hibiclens for more than five minutes, a digital block was performed with 1:1 solution of Marcaine 0.5% and Lidocaine 2%. Under sterile technique the nail was removed, revealing a transverse V-shaped nail bed laceration. No crepitus was noted. The laceration was irrigated with saline and Hibiclens solution, and the nail bed laceration was repaired with #5-0 Vicryl x 3. The nail plate was reattached in the eponychial fold and secured with three #4-0 nylon sutures. The wound was cleaned and a bulky dressing was applied.
    The correct CPT code(s) to report this service would be:

    A. 11760
    B. 11730, 11760
    C. 01999, 11730, 11760
    D. 01999, 11760, 11730-51

39. Using an ophthalmic endoscope, a physician exchanges a patient's intraocular lenses. The appropriate code for this procedure is

    A. 66986, 66990
    B. 66985, 66990
    C. 66986
    D. 66985

40. A surgeon, while excising a suspicious pigmented lesion on a patient's calf, makes an incision of about 5 cm. The lesion is found to measure more than 5 cm, and retraction of the skin edges does not allow primary closure. After extensive skin undermining, the wound repair was completed. The most appropriate coding for this procedure would be

    A. 11606, 13121
    B. 11606
    C. 11606, 12032
    D. 11600, 13121

41. A patient is prepared for surgery to repair a spigelian hernia. Before anesthesia is administered, the physician decides the procedure should not be performed. This should

    A. not be coded
    B. be coded as 49590, with a an attached explanatory note
    C. 49590-52
    D. 49590-73

42. A patient reports to emergency room after a fall. The ER physician performs a layered closure of a 3 cm laceration of the patient's upper arm, and a simple suture of a .5 cm laceration of the patient's calf. The most appropriate coding for these procedures would be

    A. 99281, 12301, 12001
    B. 99281-25, 12302, 12001-59
    C. 12302, 12001-58
    D. 12302, 12001-59

43. A physician performed a preoperative placement of a needle localization wire in a patient's breast under radiological supervision. The code for this procedure is

    A. 19290
    B. 19290, 19291
    C. 19290, 76096
    D. 19290 x 2

44. The modifier LC, attached to a surgical code, means that the procedure

    A. was performed on the left coronary artery
    B. was performed on the left side
    C. is an ambulatory surgical center service
    D. is expected to be denied as not reasonable and necessary

45. Prior to performing a tympanostomy in both ears, a physician removed the impacted cerumen in the right ear in order to enable surgery. The most appropriate CPT coding for these procedures is

    A. 69210-R, 69433
    B. 69433-50, 69210-59
    C. 69433-50
    D. 69210-59, 69433-50

46. Code for a right modified radical mastectomy, including the axillary lymph nodes, without any muscles.

    A. 19160
    B. 19200
    C. 19220
    D. 19240

Miscellaneous

47. A 70-year-old patient, who has breast cancer herself and a family history of colon cancer, undergoes a screening colonoscopy in her physician's office. The most appropriate code for this procedure is

    A. G0121-53
    B. G0105, 45378
    C. G0105
    D. G0121

48. The modifier GN, attached to a surgical code, indicates a(n)

    A. screening mammogram and diagnostic mammogram on the same patient on the same day
    B. service delivered under an outpatient occupational therapy plan of care
    C. item or service statutorily excluded from Medicare coverage
    D. service delivered under an outpatient speech language pathology plan of care

49. Code for 48 hours of prolonged extracorporeal circulation for cardiopulmonary insufficiency.

    A. 33960
    B. 33960 x2
    C. 33961 x 2
    D. 33960;33961

50. What is the term for a diagnostic test that uses a specific antibody or antigen to detect the presence of an analyte?

    A. Immunoassay
    B. Assay
    C. Panel
    D. Series

KEY (CORRECT ANSWERS)

1. C	11. C	21. D	31. C	41. D
2. C	12. C	22. A	32. B	42. B
3. B	13. A	23. A	33. A	43. C
4. B	14. C	24. A	34. A	44. A
5. B	15. D	25. B	35. D	45. C
6. A	16. A	26. C	36. B	46. D
7. B	17. C	27. C	37. B	47. C
8. D	18. D	28. D	38. A	48. D
9. A	19. A	29. C	39. A	49. D
10. C	20. A	30. B	40. A	50. A

TEST 2

DIRECTIONS: Each question or incomplete statement is followed by several suggested answers or completions. Select the one that BEST answers the question or completes the statement. *PRINT THE LETTER OF THE CORRECT ANSWER IN THE SPACE AT THE RIGHT.*

Medical Terminology

1. In medical terms, the suffix "-oid" means   1.____

    A. of or pertaining to
    B. straight
    C. around or near
    D. like or resembling

2. A cholecystectomy is an excision of the   2.____

    A. spleen
    B. gallbladder
    C. renal gland
    D. liver

3. In medical terminology, a diminutive suffix forms a word that designates a small version   3.____
   of an object indicated by the word root. Which of the following is NOT a diminutive suffix?

    A. -ole
    B. -ula
    C. -ina
    D. -icle

4. The pineal gland is a   4.____

    A. part of the brain located beneath teh cerebral hemispheres and next to the third ventricle, which serves as a relay station for nerve impulses in the brain.
    B. region of the brain located below the thalamus, forming the major portion of the ventral region of the diencephalon.
    C. small reddish-gray body that is part of the epithalamus
    D. pea-sized endocrine gland that sits in a small, bony cavity at the base of the brain

5. Myasthenia gravis is a condition of the   5.____

    A. muscles
    B. lymph
    C. nerves
    D. endocrine system

6. The medical term that describes an inflammation of the salivary gland is   6.____

    A. sialitis
    B. linguosis
    C. stomatitis
    D. gingivitis

7. The medical abbreviation AD is often used to designate the

    A. left eye
    B. right eye
    C. left ear
    D. right ear

8. The medical term that denotes a decrease or insufficiency of white blood cells is

    A. hypoleukocytis
    B. leukans
    C. leukocytopenia
    D. leukocytemia

9. Salpingitis is a word that refers to inflammation of the

    A. ovary
    B. uterus
    C. vagina
    D. Fallopian tube

ICD-9-CM

10. Code for gangrenous necrotizing fascitis. The culture grew staphylococci.

    A. 728.86, 041.10
    B. 728.9, 785.4, 041.10
    C. 738.4, 041.10
    D. 728.86, 785.4, 041.10

11. Code for a history of a cerebral artery occlusion with infarction with residuals of hemiplegia and aphasia.

    A. 434.91, 342.90, 784.3
    B. 438.20
    C. 438.20, 438.11
    D. 784.3, 434.91

12. A woman reports for a scheduled mammogram. She has been flagged as a high-risk patient because her mother had breast cancer. The mammogram is conducted and reveals no abnormalities. What is the principal diagnosis code?

    A. V76.1
    B. V76.11
    C. V76.12
    D. 611.72

13. A patient reports to the emergency room with intense chest pains, shortness of breath, and a dry cough. The patient was recently diagnosed with gonorrhea. The physician diagnoses him with acute gonococcal pericarditis.
    The best code for this diagnosis is

    A. 420.90, 098.80
    B. 098.83
    C. 420.0, 098.83
    D. 420.99

14. A patient has systemic lupus erythematosus, which has caused her to suffer from chronic nephritis. What diagnosis codes should be reported?

    A. 710, 581.81
    B. 583.81, 710.0
    C. 582.81, 710.0
    D. 710.0, 582.81

15. For coding purposes, an excisional debridement of a burn wound that is NOT performed by a physician would be coded

    A. 86.22
    B. 86.28
    C. 85.69
    D. 93.57

16. A patient was standing on a stepladder on his patio, pruning bushes, when he falls onto the patio and sustains a brain stem injury. He loses consciousness and never regains consciousness, and dies within 48 hours. The most accurate code for this episode is

    A. 854.05, E881.0, E849.0
    B. 854.15, E884.2
    C. 854.04, E882.0, E849.7
    D. 854.05, E881.0

17. A burn victim has been admitted to the hospital very recently, and in her diagnosis the physician has not specified the site of the burn. The coder should assign a code from category

    A. 942
    B. 946
    C. 948
    D. 949

Payment Methodologies

18. Which of the following is a key characteristic of the Ambulatory Payment Classification (APC)?

    A. Payment for inpatient services
    B. Payment based on fee schedule
    C. Assignment determined through HCPCS system
    D. Fee-for-service payment

19. On CMS 1450, the patient control number is entered in field

    A. 1a
    B. 1
    C. 3
    D. 12

20. The purpose of pass-through payments is to

    A. supplement the cost for payment under the Ambulatory Payment Classification (APC)
    B. reduce the hospital charges for each item billed by using the hospital cost-to-charges ratio
    C. reduce standard payments amounts for an Ambulatory Payment Classification (APC)
    D. eliminate payments for drugs and biologicals

21. Which of the following would be a valid "place of service" code for field 24b of CMS 1500?

    A. 32
    B. 27
    C. 47
    D. 11

22. A patient's medical record number is entered in form locator (FL) _____ of CMS 1450.

    A. 1
    B. 5
    C. 23
    D. 35

23. Each of the following services is covered by Part B Medicare, EXCEPT

    A. home health care
    B. outpatient hospital care
    C. inpatient hospital care
    D. physician's services

24. Of the following, the best definition of "revenue center" is

    A. a system for reimbursing inpatient hospital costs
    B. a facility cost center for which a separate charge is billed on an institutional claim
    C. any facility, inpatient or outpatient, that participates in Medicare
    D. the standard for measuring the value of medical services provided by physicians

25. A procedure code with the status modifier _____ will result in payment for the item, drug or biological in addition to the APC reimbursement for the service performed.

    A. A
    B. B
    C. G
    D. X

General CPT

26. Which of the following is "10-day" CPT code?

    A. 12057
    B. 10060
    C. 15302
    D. 17108

27. Code for an anterior spinal fusion of L5-S1, with cages and bone grafting, for a spinal surgeon and a general surgeon working together. The general surgeon worked together on the anterior fusion, while assisting on the cages and grafts. The correct way to code for the general surgeon's participation in this operation would be:

    A. 22558-62
    B. 22558-62, 22851-62, 20937-62
    C. 22558-80, 22851-80, 20937-80
    D. 22558-62, 22851-80, 20937-80

28. The correct way to code for 90 minutes of critical care is

    A. 99291, 99175
    B. 99291, 99292
    C. 99295, 99292
    D. 99292, 99292, 99292

29. The code that should be used for arthroplasty of the toe is

    A. 28108
    B. 28124
    C. 28510
    D. 28899

30. Category II CPT codes are

    A. supplemental tracking codes that can be used for performance measurement, but not reimbursement
    B. alphanumeric codes intended to allow data tracking for emerging technology
    C. codes that are combined within the global surgical period
    D. new procedure codes that have been added since the most recent edition of the CPT manual

31. When a CPT code is "technical service only," it means that

    A. MOD-TC must always be added
    B. only the facility (hospital), would bill for services
    C. if the hospital wants to bill for professional services also, it should submit code MOD-26
    D. only the provider (physician) would bill for services

32. Code for the dilation of the esophagus with a 25-mm balloon.

    A. 43201
    B. 43220
    C. 43249
    D. 43456

33. Which of the following is a case management code?

    A. 99631
    B. 99490
    C. 99210
    D. 99815

34. For the initial evaluation of a problem for which a procedure is performed, modifier _____ is used.

    A. 24
    B. 25
    C. 32
    D. 51

35. Code for retrograde catheterization of the left heart from the femoral artery.

    A. 93501
    B. 93510
    C. 93511
    D. 93514

Surgical Procedures

36. A surgeon performed a bilateral levator resection for upper lid ptosis. The appropriate code is

    A. 67904 x 2
    B. 67904R, 67904L
    C. 67904-50
    D. 67904-51

37. Samantha, a 40-year-old with documented fibroids and anemia, scheduled surgery with her gynecologist. An ultrasound also identified a left ovarian cyst. Adriana underwent a supracervical hysterectomy, as had been discussed, but her Fallopian tubes and ovaries were left in place. At the same time, the gynecologist opened and drained the ovarian cyst and sent a biopsy of the cyst wall to pathology. She then removed the cyst capsule from Samantha's ovary. What code(s) should be reported for this service?

    A. 58180, 58925-51
    B. 58180, 58925-59
    C. 58180, 58925
    D. 58180

38. A patient underwent a stereotactic biopsy of her left breast. Following local anesthesia with approximately 5 cc of 1% Lidocaine, a small incision was made in the skin. An 11-gauge mammotome was inserted through the incision to the level of the microcalcifications following the stereotactic coordinates. Stereotactic images were obtained to confirm accurate positioning of the mammotome probe. The mechanical cutter was then activated, tissue was cut, excised and transported through the mammotome probe to the collection chamber. A Micromark sterile surgical clip was injected at the conclusion of the procedure to mark the biopsy site in the event of future surgical excision and to monitor future mammograms.
The correct CPT code(s) for reporting this service would be

    A. 19103,19295-59
    B. J0704, 19103-LT, 19295-LT
    C. 19103-LT, 19295-LT
    D. 19103

39. A surgeon removes two malignant lesions—one measuring 3.0 cm, the other 1.8 cm—from a patient's hand, and follows each excision with a simple closure. The most appropriate way to code for this procedure is

    A. 11623 x 2,12301 x 2
    B. 11623, 16223-59, 12301 x 2
    C. 11623, 16222
    D. There is not enough information to code for this procedure.

40. A surgeon performs an anterior cervical decompression and fusion while using an operating microscope with placement of Atlantis plating and a fibular strut allograft. The correct code for this procedure is

    A. 22554, 63075-51, 22845, 20931
    B. 22554, 63075-51, 22845, 69990, 20931
    C. 22554, 63075, 22845, 69990, 20931
    D. 22554, 63075, 22845

41. Extensive enterolysis of adhesions is performed during an inguinal hernial repair performed on a 55 year-old male using a mesh prosthesis. The appropriate code(s) to report this service is/are:

    A. 49505-22
    B. 49650-22
    C. 49505, 44005-59
    D. 49505, 49568, 44005-59

42. A patient with a congenital cleft lip had it repaired with closure of the alveolar ridge, which included a bone graft to the alveolar ridge. In addition, the nose was repaired, which involved a columellar lengthening of the septum that required a bone graft. Code for these procedures.

    A. 30462, 42210-50, 21210-50
    B. 30462, 42210-51, 21210-51
    C. 30420, 42210, 21210
    D. 30462, 42210, 21210

43. Code for arthrotomy of the wrist joint with biopsy and synovectomy. 43.____

    A. 25100, 25105-51
    B. 25105
    C. 25101
    D. 25100, 25105

44. During an office visit, a physician removes 24 small skin tags from a patient's back and neck. The most appropriate procedural code for this is 44.____

    A. 11200-51
    B. 11200
    C. 11200, 11201
    D. 11200, 11201-51

45. After performing a cystourethroscopy, a surgeon places an indwelling ureteral stent. Later that evening, the patient returns to the operating room to have the stent removed by the same surgeon. The modifier that should be used with the code for the removal is 45.____

    A. 51
    B. 58
    C. 76
    D. 78

46. Using two separate incisions, a hand surgeon removes two separate benign lesions, each measuring about 1.0 cm, from a patient's left hand. The appropriate procedure code would be 46.____

    A. 11401 x 2
    B. 11401
    C. 11400, 11401
    D. 11401, 11401-59

Miscellaneous

47. A ligation is a procedure that involves 47.____

    A. forcing a fluid into a vessel or cavity
    B. binding or tying off
    C. uniting parts by stitching them together
    D. suturing

48. The conjunctivo-Tarso Muller resection is a procedure that 48.____

    A. corrects for strabismus
    B. straightens a clubfoot
    C. repairs a ptotic upper eyelid
    D. minimizes scar tissue after grafts

49. Which of the following is an add-on code?

    A. 15201
    B. 28900
    C. 01951
    D. 42999

50. Curettage is a mode of treatment that involves

    A. puncturing an organ or tissue
    B. the removal of part or all of an organ
    C. removing a small piece of living tissue
    D. scraping away body tissue

KEY (CORRECT ANSWERS)

1. D	11. C	21. D	31. B	41. B
2. B	12. B	22. C	32. B	42. B
3. C	13. B	23. C	33. A	43. B
4. C	14. D	24. B	34. B	44. C
5. A	15. B	25. C	35. B	45. B
6. A	16. A	26. B	36. B	46. A
7. D	17. C	27. D	37. B	47. B
8. C	18. C	28. B	38. C	48. C
9. D	19. C	29. D	39. C	49. A
10. D	20. B	30. A	40. A	50. D

READING COMPREHENSION
UNDERSTANDING AND INTERPRETING WRITTEN MATERIAL
EXAMINATION SECTION
TEST 1

Questions 1-8.

DIRECTIONS: Each question or incomplete statement is followed by several suggested answers or completions. Select the one that BEST answers the question or completes the statement. *PRINT THE LETTER OF THE CORRECT ANSWER IN THE SPACE AT THE RIGHT.*

Questions 1 and 2.

DIRECTIONS: Your answers to Questions 1 and 2 must be based ONLY on the information given in the following paragraph.

Hospitals maintained wholly by public taxation may treat only those compensation cases which are emergencies and may not treat such emergency cases longer than the emergency exists; provided, however, that these restrictions shall not be applicable where there is not available a hospital other than a hospital maintained wholly by taxation.

1. According to the above paragraph, compensation cases

   A. are regarded as emergency cases by hospitals maintained wholly by public taxation
   B. are seldom treated by hospitals maintained wholly by public taxation
   C. are treated mainly by privately endowed hospitals
   D. may be treated by hospitals maintained wholly by public taxation if they are emergencies

2. According to the above paragraph, it is MOST reasonable to conclude that where a privately endowed hospital is available,

   A. a hospital supported wholly by public taxation may treat emergency compensation cases only so long as the emergency exists
   B. a hospital supported wholly by public taxation may treat any compensation cases
   C. a hospital supported wholly by public taxation must refer emergency compensation cases to such a hospital
   D. the restrictions regarding the treatment of compensation cases by a tax-supported hospital are not wholly applicable

Questions 3-7.

DIRECTIONS: Answer Questions 3 through 7 ONLY according to the information given in the following passage.

THE MANUFACTURE OF LAUNDRY SOAP

The manufacture of soap is not a complicated process. Soap is a fat or an oil, plus an alkali, water and salt. The alkali used in making commercial laundry soap is caustic soda. The salt used is the same as common table salt. A fat is generally an animal product that is not a liquid at room temperature. If heated, it becomes a liquid. An oil is generally liquid at room temperature. If the temperature is lowered, the oil becomes a solid just like ordinary fat.

At the soap plant, a huge tank five stories high, called a *kettle,* is first filled part way with fats and then the alkali and water are added. These ingredients are then heated and boiled together. Salt is then poured into the top of the boiling solution; and as the salt slowly sinks down through the mixture, it takes with it the glycerine which comes from the melted fats. The product which finally comes from the kettle is a clear soap which has a moisture content of about 34%. This clear soap is then chilled so that more moisture is driven out. As a result, the manufacturer finally ends up with a commercial laundry soap consisting of 88% clear soap and only 12% moisture.

3. An ingredient used in making laundry soap is

    A. table sugar
    B. potash
    C. glycerine
    D. caustic soda

4. According to the above passage, a difference between fats and oils is that fats

    A. cost more than oils
    B. are solid at room temperature
    C. have less water than oils
    D. are a liquid animal product

5. According to the above passage, the MAIN reason for using salt in the manufacture of soap is to

    A. make the ingredients boil together
    B. keep the fats in the kettle melted
    C. remove the glycerine
    D. prevent the loss of water from the soap

6. According to the passage, the purpose of chilling the clear soap is to

    A. stop the glycerine from melting
    B. separate the alkali from the fats
    C. make the oil become solid
    D. get rid of more moisture

7. According to the passage, the percentage of moisture in commercial laundry soap is

    A. 12%   B. 34%   C. 66%   D. 88%

8. The x-ray has gone into business. Developed primarily to aid in diagnosing human ills, the machine now works in packing plants, in foundries, in service stations, and in a dozen ways to contribute to precision and accuracy in industry.
   The above statement means *most nearly* that the x-ray

   A. was first developed to aid business
   B. is of more help to business than it is to medicine
   C. is being used to improve the functioning of business
   D. is more accurate for packing plants than it is for foundries

8.____

Questions 9-25.

DIRECTIONS: Each question consists of a statement. You are to indicate whether the statement is TRUE (T) or FALSE (F). *PRINT THE LETTER OF THE CORRECT ANSWER IN THE SPACE AT THE RIGHT.*

Questions 9-12.

DIRECTIONS: Read the paragraph below about *shock* and then answer Questions 9 through 12 according to the information given in the paragraph.

SHOCK

While not found in all injuries, shock is present in all serious injuries caused by accidents. During shock, the normal activities of the body slow down. This partly explains why one of the signs of shock is a pale, cold skin, since insufficient blood goes to the body parts during shock.

9. If the injury caused by an accident is serious, shock is sure to be present.   9.____

10. In shock, the heart beats faster than normal.   10.____

11. The face of a person suffering from shock is usually red and flushed.   11.____

12. Not enough blood goes to different parts of the body during shock.   12.____

Questions 13-18.

DIRECTIONS: Questions 13 through 18, inclusive, are to be answered SOLELY on the basis of the information contained in the following statement and NOT upon any other information you may have.

Blood transfusions are given to patients at the hospital upon recommendation of the physicians attending such cases. The physician fills out a *Request for Blood Transfusion* form in duplicate and sends both copies to the Medical Director's office, where a list is maintained of persons called *donors* who desire to sell their blood for transfusions. A suitable donor is selected, and the transfusion is given. Donors are, in many instances, medical students and employees of the hospital. Donors receive twenty-five dollars for each transfusion.

13. According to the above paragraph, a blood donor is paid twenty-five dollars for each transfusion.   13.____

14. According to the above paragraph, only medical students and employees of the hospital are selected as blood donors. 14.___

15. According to the above paragraph, the *Request for Blood Transfusion* form is filled out by the patient and sent to the Medical Director's office. 15.___

16. According to the above paragraph, a list of blood donors is maintained in the Medical Director's office. 16.___

17. According to the above paragraph, cases for which the attending physicians recommend blood transfusions are usually emergency cases. 17.___

18. According to the above paragraph, one copy of the *Request for Blood Transfusion* form is kept by the patient and one copy is sent to the Medical Director's office. 18.___

Questions 19-25.

DIRECTIONS: Questions 19 through 25, inclusive, are to be answered SOLELY on the basis of the information contained in the following passage and NOT upon any other information you may have.

Before being admitted to a hospital ward, a patient is first interviewed by the Admitting Clerk, who records the patient's name, age, sex, race, birthplace, and mother's maiden name. This clerk takes all of the money and valuables that the patient has on his person. A list of the valuables is written on the back of the envelope in which the valuables are afterwards placed. Cash is counted and placed in a separate envelope, and the amount of money and the name of the patient are written on the outside of the envelope. Both envelopes are sealed, fastened together, and placed in a compartment of a safe.

An orderly then escorts the patient to a dressing room where the patient's clothes are removed and placed in a bundle. A tag bearing the patient's name is fastened to the bundle. A list of the contents of the bundle is written on property slips, which are made out in triplicate. The information contained on the outside of the envelopes containing the cash and valuables belonging to the patient is also copied on the property slips.

According to the above passage,

19. patients are escorted to the dressing room by the Admitting Clerk. 19.___

20. the patient's cash and valuables are placed together in one envelope. 20.___

21. the number of identical property slips that are made out when a patient is being admitted to a hospital ward is three. 21.___

22. the full names of both parents of a patient are recorded by the Admitting Clerk before a patient is admitted to a hospital ward. 22.___

23. the amount of money that a patient has on his person when admitted to the hospital is entered on the patient's property slips. 23.___

24. an orderly takes all the money and valuables that a patient has on his person. 24.___

25. the patient's name is placed on the tag that is attached to the bundle containing the patient's clothing. 25.___

KEY (CORRECT ANSWERS)

1. D
2. A
3. D
4. B
5. C

6. D
7. A
8. C
9. T
10. F

11. F
12. T
13. T
14. F
15. F

16. T
17. T
18. F
19. F
20. F

21. T
22. F
23. T
24. F
25. T

TEST 2

DIRECTIONS: Each question or incomplete statement is followed by several suggested answers or completions. Select the one that BEST answers the question or completes the statement. *PRINT THE LETTER OF THE CORRECT ANSWER IN THE SPACE AT THE RIGHT.*

Questions 1-4.

DIRECTIONS: Questions 1 through 4 are to be answered in accordance with the following paragraphs.

One fundamental difference between the United States health care system and the health care systems of some European countries is the way that hospital charges for long-term illnesses affect their citizens.

In European countries such as England, Sweden, and Germany, citizens can face, without fear, hospital charges due to prolonged illness, no matter how substantial they may be. Citizens of these nations are required to pay nothing when they are hospitalized, for they have prepaid their treatment as taxpayers when they were well and were earning incomes.

On the other hand, the United States citizen, in spite of the growth of payments by third parties which include private insurance carriers as well as public resources, has still to shoulder 40 percent of hospital care costs, while his private insurance contributes only 25 percent and public resources the remaining 35 percent.

Despite expansion of private health insurance and social legislation in the United States, out-of-pocket payments for hospital care by individuals have steadily increased. Such payments, currently totalling $23 billion, are nearly twice as high as ten years ago.

Reform is inevitable and, when it comes, will have to reconcile sharply conflicting interests. Hospital staffs are demanding higher and higher wages. Hospitals are under pressure by citizens, who as patients demand more and better services but who as taxpayers or as subscribers to hospital insurance plans, are reluctant to pay the higher cost of improved care. An acceptable reconciliation of these interests has so far eluded legislators and health administrators in the United States.

1. According to the above passage, the one of the following which is an ADVANTAGE that citizens of England, Sweden, and Germany have over United States citizens is that, when faced with long-term illness, 1.___

    A. the amount of out-of-pocket payments made by these European citizens is small when compared to out-of-pocket payments made by United States citizens
    B. European citizens have no fear of hospital costs no matter how great they may be
    C. more efficient and reliable hospitals are available to the European citizen than is available to the United States citizens
    D. a greater range of specialized hospital care is available to the European citizens than is available to the United States citizens

2. According to the above passage, reform of the United States system of health care must reconcile all of the following EXCEPT

   A. attempts by health administrators to provide improved hospital care
   B. taxpayers' reluctance to pay for the cost of more and better hospital services
   C. demands by hospital personnel for higher wages
   D. insurance subscribers' reluctance to pay the higher costs of improved hospital care

3. According to the above passage, the out-of-pocket payments for hospital care that individuals made ten years ago was APPROXIMATELY _____ billion.

   A. $32   B. $23   C. $12   D. $3

4. According to the above passage, the GREATEST share of the costs of hospital care in the United States is paid by

   A. United States citizens
   B. private insurance carriers
   C. public resources
   D. third parties

Questions 5-8.

DIRECTIONS: Questions 5 through 8 are to be answered SOLELY on the basis of the information contained in the following passage.

Effective cost controls have been difficult to establish in most hospitals in the United States. Ways must be found to operate hospitals with reasonable efficiency without sacrificing quality and in a manner that will reduce the amount of personal income now being spent on health care and the enormous drain on national resources. We must adopt a new public objective of providing higher quality health care at significantly lower cost. One step that can be taken to achieve this goal is to carefully control capital expenditures for hospital construction and expansion. Perhaps the way to start is to declare a moratorium on all hospital construction and to determine the factors that should be considered in deciding whether a hospital should be built. Such factors might include population growth, distance to the nearest hospital, availability of medical personnel, and hospital bed shortage.

A second step to achieve the new objective is to increase the ratio of out-of-hospital patient to in-hospital patient care. This can be done by using separate health care facilities other than hospitals to attract patients who have increasingly been going to hospital clinics and overcrowding them. Patients should instead identify with a separate health care facility to keep them out of hospitals.

A third step is to require better hospital operating rules and controls. This step might include the review of a doctor's performance by other doctors, outside professional evaluations of medical practice, and required refresher courses and re-examinations for doctors. Other measures might include obtaining mandatory second opinions on the need for surgery in order to avoid unnecessary surgery, and outside review of work rules and procedures to eliminate unnecessary testing of patients.

A fourth step is to halt the construction and public subsidizing of new medical schools and to fill whatever needs exist in professional coverage by emphasizing the medical training of physicians with specialities that are in short supply and by providing a better geographic distribution of physicians and surgeons.

5. According to the above passage, providing higher quality health care at lower cost can be achieved by the

   A. greater use of out-of-hospital facilities
   B. application of more effective cost controls on doctors' fees
   C. expansion of improved in-hospital patient care services at hospital clinics
   D. development of more effective training programs in hospital administration

6. According to the above passage, the one of the following which should be taken into account in determining if a hospital should be constructed is the

   A. number of out-of-hospital health care facilities
   B. availability of public funds to subsidize construction
   C. number of hospitals under construction
   D. availability of medical personnel

7. According to the above passage, it is IMPORTANT to operate hospitals efficiently because

   A. they are currently in serious financial difficulties
   B. of the need to reduce the amount of personal income going to health care
   C. the quality of health care services has deteriorated
   D. of the need to increase productivity goals to take care of the growing population in the United States

8. According to the above passage, which one of the following approaches is MOST LIKELY to result in better operating rules and controls in hospitals?

   A. Allocating doctors to health care facilities on the basis of patient population
   B. Equalizing the workloads of doctors
   C. Establishing a physician review board to evaluate the performance of other physicians
   D. Eliminating unnecessary outside review of patient testing

Questions 9-14.

DIRECTIONS: Questions 9 through 14 are to be answered SOLELY on the basis of the information contained in the following passage.

The United States today is the only major industrial nation in the world without a system of national health insurance or a national health service. Instead, we have placed our prime reliance on private enterprise and private health insurance to meet the need. Yet, in a recent year, of the 180 million Americans under 65 years of age, 34 million had no hospital insurance, 38 million had no surgical insurance, 63 million had no out-patient x-ray and laboratory insurance, 94 million had no insurance for prescription drugs, and 103 million had no insurance for physician office visits or home visits. Some 35 million Americans under the age of 65 had no health insurance whatsoever. Some 64 million additional Americans under age 65 had health insurance coverage that was less than that provided to the aged under Medicare.

Despite more than three decades of enormous growth, the private health insurance industry today pays benefits equal to only one-third of the total cost of private health care, leaving the rest to be borne by the patient—essentially the same ratio which held true a decade ago. Moreover, nearly all private health insurance is limited; it provides partial benefits, not comprehensive benefits; acute care, not preventive care; it siphons off the young and healthy, and ignores the poor and medically indigent. The typical private carrier usually pays only the cost of hospital care, forcing physicians and patients alike to resort to wasteful and inefficient use of hospital facilities, thereby giving further impetus to the already soaring costs of hospital care. Valuable hospital beds are used for routine tests and examinations. Unnecessary hospitalization, unnecessary surgery, and unnecessarily extended hospital stays are encouraged. These problems are exacerbated by the fact that administrative costs of commercial carriers are substantially higher than they are for Blue Shield, Blue Cross, or Medicare.

9. According to the above passage, the PROPORTION of total private health care costs paid by private health insurance companies today as compared to ten years ago has

    A. *increased* by approximately one-third
    B. *remained* practically the same
    C. *increased* by approximately two-thirds
    D. *decreased* by approximately one-third

10. According to the above passage, the one of the following which has contributed MOST to wasteful use of hospital facilities is the

    A. increased emphasis on preventive health care
    B. practice of private carriers of providing comprehensive health care benefits
    C. increased hospitalization of the elderly and the poor
    D. practice of a number of private carriers of paying only for hospital care costs

11. Based on the information in the above passage, which one of the following patients would be LEAST likely to receive benefits from a typical private health insurance plan?
    A

    A. young patient who must undergo an emergency appendectomy
    B. middle-aged patient who needs a costly series of x-ray and laboratory tests for diagnosis of gastrointestinal complaints
    C. young patient who must visit his physician weekly for treatment of a chronic skin disease
    D. middle-aged patient who requires extensive cancer surgery

12. Which one of the following is the MOST accurate inference that can be drawn from the above passage?

    A. Private health insurance has failed to fully meet the health care needs of Americans.
    B. Most Americans under age 65 have health insurance coverage better than that provided to the elderly under Medicare.
    C. Countries with a national health service are likely to provide poorer health care for their citizens than do countries that rely primarily on private health insurance.
    D. Hospital facilities in the United States are inadequate to meet the nation's health care needs.

13. Of the total number of Americans under age 65, what percentage belonged in the combined category of persons with NO health insurance or health insurance less than that provided to the aged under Medicare?

    A. 19%   B. 36%   C. 55%   D. 65%

14. According to the above passage, the one of the following types of health insurance which covered the SMALLEST number of Americans under age 65 was

    A. hospital insurance
    B. surgical insurance
    C. insurance for prescription drugs
    D. insurance for physician office or home visits

Questions 15-17.

DIRECTIONS: Questions 15 through 17 are to be answered SOLELY on the basis of the information contained in the following passage.

Statistical studies have demonstrated that disease and mortality rates are higher among the poor than among the more affluent members of our society. Periodic surveys conducted by the United States Public Health Service continue to document a higher prevalence of infectious and chronic diseases within low income families. While the basic life style and living conditions of the poor are to a considerable extent responsible for this less favorable health status, there are indications that the kind of health care received by the poor also plays a significant role. The poor are less likely to be aware of the concepts and practices of scientific medicine and less likely to seek health care when they need it. Moreover, they are discouraged from seeking adequate health care by the depersonalization, disorganization, and inadequate emphasis on preventive care which characterize the health care most often provided for them.

To achieve the objective of better health care for the poor, the following approaches have been suggested: encouraging the poor to seek preventive care as well as care for acute illness and to establish a lasting one-to-one relationship with a single physician who can treat the poor patient as a whole individual; sufficient financial subsidy to put the poor on an equal footing with *paying patients,* thereby giving them the opportunity to choose from among available health services providers; inducements to health services providers to establish public clinics in poverty areas; and legislation to provide for health education, earlier detection of disease, and coordinated health care.

15. According to the above passage, the one of the following which is a function of the United States Public Health Service is

    A. gathering data on the incidence of infectious diseases
    B. operating public health clinics in poverty areas lacking private physicians
    C. recommending legislation for the improvement of health care in the United States
    D. encouraging the poor to participate in programs aimed at the prevention of illness

16. According to the above passage, the one of the following which is MOST characteristic of the health care currently provided for the poor is that it

    A. aims at establishing clinics in poverty areas
    B. enables the poor to select the health care they want through the use of financial subsidies
    C. places insufficient stress on preventive health care
    D. over-emphasizes the establishment of a one-to-one relationship between physician and patient

16._____

17. The above passage IMPLIES that the poor lack the financial resources to

    A. obtain adequate health insurance coverage
    B. select from among existing health services
    C. participate in health education programs
    D. lobby for legislation aimed at improving their health care

17._____

Questions 18-20.

DIRECTIONS: Questions 18 through 20 are to be answered SOLELY on the basis of the information contained in the following passage.

The concept of *affiliation,* developed more than ten years ago, grew out of a series of studies which found evidence of faulty care, surgery of *questionable* value and other undesirable conditions in the city's municipal hospitals. The affiliation agreements signed shortly thereafter were designed to correct these deficiencies by assuring high quality medical care. In general, the agreements provided the staff and expertise of a voluntary hospital—sometimes connected with a medical school—to operate various services or, in some cases, all of the professional divisions of a specific municipal hospital. The municipal hospitals have paid for these services, which last year cost the city $200 million, the largest single expenditure of the Health and Hospitals Corporation. In addition, the municipal hospitals have provided to the voluntary hospitals such facilities as free space for laboratories and research. While some experts agree that affiliation has resulted in improvements in some hospital care, they contend that many conditions that affiliation was meant to correct still exist. In addition, accountability procedures between the Corporation and voluntary hospitals are said to be so inadequate that audits of affiliation contracts of the past five years revealed that there may be more than $200 million in charges for services by the voluntary hospitals which have not been fully substantiated. Consequently, the Corporation has proposed that future agreements provide accountability in terms of funds, services supplied, and use of facilities by the voluntary hospitals.

18. According to the above passage, *affiliation* may BEST be defined as an agreement whereby

    A. voluntary hospitals pay for the use of municipal hospital facilities
    B. voluntary and municipal hospitals work to eliminate duplication of services
    C. municipal hospitals pay voluntary hospitals for services performed
    D. voluntary and municipal hospitals transfer patients to take advantage of specialized services

18._____

19. According to the above passage, the MAIN purpose for setting up the *affiliation* agreement was to

   A. supplement the revenues of municipal hospitals
   B. improve the quality of medical care in municipal hospitals
   C. reduce operating costs in municipal hospitals
   D. increase the amount of space available to municipal hospitals

20. According to the above passage, inadequate accountability procedures have resulted in

   A. unsubstantiated charges for services by the voluntary hospitals
   B. emphasis on research rather than on patient care in municipal hospitals
   C. unsubstantiated charges for services by the municipal hospitals
   D. economic losses to voluntary hospitals

Questions 21-25.

DIRECTIONS: Questions 21 through 25 are to be answered SOLELY on the basis of the information contained in the following passage.

The payment for medical services covered under the Outpatient Medical Insurance Plan (OMI) may be made, by OMI, directly to a physician or to the OMI patient. If the physician and the patient agree that the physician is to receive payment directly from OMI, the payment will be officially assigned to the physician; this is the assignment method. If payment is not assigned, the patient receives payment directly from OMI based on an itemized bill he submits, regardless of whether or not he has already paid his physician.

When a physician accepts assignment of the payment for medical services, he agrees that total charges will not be more than the allowed charge determined by the OMI carrier administering the program. In such cases, the OMI patient pays any unmet part of the $85 annual deductible, plus 10 percent of the remaining charges to the physician. In unassigned claims, the patient is responsible for the total amount charged by the physician. The patient will then be reimbursed by the program 90 percent of the allowed charges in excess of the annual deductible.

The rates of acceptance of assignments provide a measure of how many OMI patients are spared *administrative participation* in the program. Because physicians are free to accept or reject assignments, the rate in which assignments are made provide a general indication of the medical community's satisfaction with the OMI program, especially with the level of amounts paid by the program for specific services and the promptness of payment.

21. According to the above passage, in order for a physician to receive payment directly from OMI for medical services to an OMI patient, the physician would have to accept the assignment of payment, to have the consent of the patient, AND to

   A. submit to OMI a paid itemized bill
   B. collect from the patient 90% of the total bill
   C. collect from the patient the total amount of the charges for his services, a portion of which he will later reimburse the patient
   D. agree that his charges for services to the patient will not exceed the amount allowed by the program

22. According to the above passage, if a physician accepts assignment of payment, the patient pays

   A. the total amount charged by the physician and is reimbursed by the program for 90 percent of the allowed charges in excess of the applicable deductible
   B. any unmet part of the $85 annual deductible, plus 90 percent of the remaining charges
   C. the total amount charged by the physician and is reimbursed by the program for 10 percent of the allowed charges in excess of the $85 annual deductible
   D. any unmet part of the $85 annual deductible, plus 10 percent of the remaining charges

22.____

23. A physician has accepted the assignment of payment for charges to an OMI patient. The physician's charges, all of which are allowed under OMI, amount to $115. This is the first time the patient has been eligible for OMI benefits and the first time the patient has received services from this physician.
According to the above passage, the patient must pay the physician

   A. $27   B. $76.50   C. $88   D. $103.50

23.____

24. In an unassigned claim, a physician's charges, all of which are allowed under OMI, amount to $165. The patient paid the physician the full amount of the bill.
If this is the FIRST time the patient has been eligible for OMI benefits, he will receive from OMI a reimbursement of

   A. $72   B. $80   C. $85   D. $93

24.____

25. According to the above passage, if the rate of acceptance of assignments by physicians is high, it is LEAST appropriate to conclude that the medical community is generally satisfied with the

   A. supplementary medical insurance program
   B. levels of amounts paid to physicians by the program
   C. number of OMI patients being spared administrative participation in the program
   D. promptness of the program in making payment for services

25.____

KEY (CORRECT ANSWERS)

1.	B	11.	C	21.	D
2.	A	12.	A	22.	D
3.	C	13.	C	23.	C
4.	D	14.	D	24.	A
5.	A	15.	A	25.	C
6.	D	16.	C		
7.	B	17.	B		
8.	C	18.	C		
9.	B	19.	B		
10.	D	20.	A		

RECORD KEEPING
EXAMINATION SECTION
TEST 1

DIRECTIONS: Each question or incomplete statement is followed by several suggested answers or completions. Select the one that BEST answers the question or completes the statement. *PRINT THE LETTER OF THE CORRECT ANSWER IN THE SPACE AT THE RIGHT.*

Questions 1-7.

DIRECTIONS: In answering Questions 1 through 7, use the following master list. For each question, determine where the name would fit on the master list. Each answer choice indicates right before or after the name in the answer choice.

    Aaron, Jane
    Armstead, Brendan
    Bailey, Charles
    Dent, Ricardo
    Grant, Mark
    Mars, Justin
    Methieu, Justine
    Parker, Cathy
    Sampson, Suzy
    Thomas, Heather

1. Schmidt, William
   A. Right before Cathy Parker
   B. Right after Heather Thomas
   C. Right after Suzy Sampson
   D. Right before Ricardo Dent

1.____

2. Asanti, Kendall
   A. Right before Jane Aaron
   B. Right after Charles Bailey
   C. Right before Justine Methieu
   D. Right after Brendan Armstead

2.____

3. O'Brien, Daniel
   A. Right after Justine Methieu
   B. Right before Jane Aaron
   C. Right after Mark Grant
   D. Right before Suzy Sampson

3.____

4. Marrow, Alison
   A. Right before Cathy Parker
   B. Right before Justin Mars
   C. Right before Mark Grant
   D. Right after Heather Thomas

4.____

5. Grantt, Marissa
   A. Right before Mark Grant
   B. Right after Mark Grant
   C. Right after Justin Mars
   D. Right before Suzy Sampson

5.____

6. Thompson, Heath
   A. Right after Justin Mars
   B. Right before Suzy Sampson
   C. Right after Heather Thomas
   D. Right before Cathy Parker

   6._____

DIRECTIONS: Before answering Question 7, add in all of the names from Questions 1 through 6. Then fit the name in alphabetical order based on the new list.

7. Francisco, Mildred
   A. Right before Mark Grant
   B. Right after Marissa Grantt
   C. Right before Alison Marrow
   D. Right after Kendall Asanti

   7._____

Questions 8-10.

DIRECTIONS: In answering Questions 8 through 10, compare each pair of names and addresses. Indicate whether they are the same or different in any way.

8. William H. Pratt, J.D.   William H. Pratt, J.D.
   Attourney at Law   Attorney at Law
   A. No differences   B. 1 difference
   C. 2 differences   D. 3 differences

   8._____

9. 1303 Theater Drive,; Apt. 3-B   1330 Theatre Drive,; Apt. 3-B
   A. No differences   B. 1 difference
   C. 2 differences   D. 3 differences

   9._____

10. Petersdorff, Briana and Mary   Petersdorff, Briana and Mary
    A. No differences   B. 1 difference
    C. 2 differences   D. 3 differences

    10._____

11. Which of the following words, if any, are misspelled?
    A. Affordable
    B. Circumstansial
    C. Legalese
    D. None of the above

    11._____

Questions 12-13.

DIRECTIONS: Questions 12 and 13 are to be answered on the basis of the following table.

Standardized Test Results for High School Students in District #1230

	English	Math	Science	Reading
High School 1	21	22	15	18
High School 2	12	16	13	15
High School 3	16	18	21	17
High School 4	19	14	15	16

The scores for each high school in the district were averaged out and listed for each subject tested. Scores of 0-10 are significantly below College Readiness Standards. 11-15 are below College Readiness, 16-20 meet College Readiness, and 21-25 are above College Readiness.

12. If the high schools need to meet or exceed in at least half the categories in order to NOT be considered "at risk," which schools are considered "at risk"?
    A. High School 2
    B. High School 3
    C. High School 4
    D. Both A and C

13. What percentage of subjects did the district as a whole meet or exceed College Readiness standards?
    A. 25%   B. 50%   C. 75%   D. 100%

Questions 14-15.

DIRECTIONS: Questions 14 and 15 are to be answered on the basis of the following information.

You have seven employees working as a part of your team: Austin, Emily, Jeremy, Christina, Martin, Harriet, and Steve. You have just sent an e-mail informing them that there will be a mandatory training session next week. To ensure that work still gets done, you are offering the training twice during the week: once on Tuesday and also on Thursday. This way half the employees will still be working while the other half attend the training. The only other issue is that Jeremy doesn't work on Tuesdays and Harriet doesn't work on Thursdays due to compressed work schedules.

14. Which of the following is a possible attendance roster for the first training session?
    A. Emily, Jeremy, Steve
    B. Steve, Christina, Harriet
    C. Harriet, Jeremy, Austin
    D. Steve, Martin, Jeremy

15. If Harriet, Christina, and Steve attend the training session on Tuesday, which of the following is a possible roster for Thursday's training session?
    A. Jeremy, Emily, and Austin
    B. Emily, Martin, and Harriet
    C. Austin, Christina, and Emily
    D. Jeremy, Emily, and Steve

Questions 16-20.

DIRECTIONS: In answering Questions 16 through 20, you will be given a word and will need to choose the answer choice that is MOST similar or different to the word.

16. Which word means the SAME as *annual*?
    A. Monthly   B. Usually   C. Yearly   D. Constantly

17. Which word means the SAME as *effort*?
    A. Energy   B. Equate   C. Cherish   D. Commence

18. Which word means the OPPOSITE of *forlorn*?
    A. Neglected   B. Lethargy   C. Optimistic   D. Astonished

19. Which word means the SAME as *risk*?
    A. Admire   B. Hazard   C. Limit   D. Hesitant

20. Which word means the OPPOSITE of *translucent*? 20.____
    A. Opaque   B. Transparent   C. Luminous   D. Introverted

21. Last year, Jamie's annual salary was $50,000. Her boss called her today 21.____
    to inform her that she would receive a 20% raise for the upcoming year. How
    much more money will Jamie receive next year?
    A. $60,000   B. $10,000   C. $1,000   D. $51,000

22. You and a co-worker work for a temp hiring agency as part of their office 22.____
    staff. You both are given 6 days off per month. How many days off are you
    and your co-worker given in a year?
    A. 24   B. 72   C. 144   D. 48

23. If Margot makes $34,000 per year and she works 40 hours per week for 23.____
    all 52 weeks, what is her hourly rate?
    A. $16.34/hour   B. $17.00/hour   C. $15.54/hour   D. $13.23/hour

24. How many dimes are there in $175.00? 24.____
    A. 175   B. 1,750   C. 3,500   D. 17,500

25. If Janey is three times as old as Emily, and Emily is 3, how old is Janey? 25.____
    A. 6   B. 9   C. 12   D. 15

KEY (CORRECT ANSWERS)

1. C 11. B
2. D 12. A
3. A 13. D
4. B 14. B
5. B 15. A

6. C 16. C
7. A 17. A
8. B 18. C
9. C 19. B
10. A 20. A

21. B
22. C
23. A
24. B
25. B

TEST 2

DIRECTIONS: Each question or incomplete statement is followed by several suggested answers or completions. Select the one that BEST answers the question or completes the statement. *PRINT THE LETTER OF THE CORRECT ANSWER IN THE SPACE AT THE RIGHT.*

Questions 1-6.

DIRECTIONS: Questions 1 through 6 are to be answered on the basis of the following information.

item	name of item to be ordered
quantity	minimum number that can be ordered
beginning amount	amount in stock at start of month
amount received	amount receiving during month
ending amount	amount in stock at end of month
amount used	amount used during month
amount to order	will need at least as much of each item as used in the previous month
unit price	cost of each unit of an item
total price	total price for the order

Item	Quantity	Beginning	Received	Ending	Amount Used	Amount to Order	Unit Price	Total Price
Pens	10	22	10	8	24	20	$0.11	$2.20
Spiral notebooks	8	30	13	12			$0.25	
Binder clips	2 boxes	3 boxes	1 box	1 box			$1.79	
Sticky notes	3 packs	12 packs	4 packs	2 packs			$1.29	
Dry erase markers	1 pack (dozen)	34 markers	8 markers	40 markers			$16.49	
Ink cartridges (printer)	1 cartridge	3 cartridges	1 cartridge	2 cartridges			$79.99	
Folders	10 folders	25 folders	15 folders	10 folders			$1.08	

1. How many packs of sticky notes were used during the month?
   A. 16   B. 10   C. 12   D. 14

2. How many folders need to be ordered for next month?
   A. 15   B. 20   C. 30   D. 40

3. What is the total price of notebooks that you will need to order?
   A. $6.00   B. $0.25   C. $4.50   D. $2.75

4. Which of the following will you spend the second most money on?
   A. Ink cartridges   B. Dry erase markers
   C. Sticky notes   D. Binder clips

5. How many packs of dry erase markers should you order?
   A. 1   B. 8   C. 12   D. 0

1.____

2.____

3.____

4.____

5.____

6. What will be the total price of the file folders you order? 6._____
   A. $20.16   B. $21.60   C. $10.80   D. $4.32

Questions 7-11.

DIRECTIONS: Questions 7 through 11 are to be answered on the basis of the following table.

Number of Car Accidents, By Location and Cause, for 2014						
	Location 1		Location 2		Location 3	
Cause	Number	Percent	Number	Percent	Number	Percent
Severe Weather	10		25		30	
Excessive Speeding	20	40	5		10	
Impaired Driving	15		15	25	8	
Miscellaneous	5		15		2	4
TOTALS	50	100	60	100	50	100

7. Which of the following is the third highest cause of accidents for all three locations? 7._____
   A. Severe Weather   B. Impaired Driving
   C. Miscellaneous   D. Excessive Speeding

8. The average number of Severe Weather accidents per week at Location 3 for the year (52 weeks) was MOST NEARLY 8._____
   A. 0.57   B. 30   C. 1   D. 1.25

9. Which location had the LARGEST percentage of accidents caused by Impaired Driving? 9._____
   A. 1   B. 2   C. 3   D. Both A and B

10. If one-third of the accidents at all three locations resulted in at least one fatality, what is the LEAST amount of deaths caused by accidents last year? 10._____
    A. 60   B. 106   C. 66   D. 53

11. What is the percentage of accidents caused by miscellaneous means from all three locations in 2014? 11._____
    A. 5%   B. 10%   C. 13%   D. 25%

12. How many pairs of the following groups of letters are exactly alike? 12._____
    ACDOBJ   ACDBOJ
    HEWBWR   HEWRWB
    DEERVS   DEERVS
    BRFQSX   BRFQSX
    WEYRVB   WEYRVB
    SPQRZA   SQRPZA

    A. 2   B. 3   C. 4   D. 5

3 (#2)

Questions 13-19.

DIRECTIONS: Questions 13 through 19 are to be answered on the basis of the following information.

In 2012, the most current information on the American population was finished. The information was compiled by 200 volunteers in each of the 50 states. The territory of Puerto Rico, a sovereign of the United States, had 25 people assigned to compile data. In February of 2010, volunteers in each state and sovereign began collecting information. In Puerto Rico, data collection finished by January 31st, 2011, while work in the United States was completed on June 30, 2012. Each volunteer gathered data on the population of their state or sovereign. When the information was compiled, volunteers sent reports to the nation's capital, Washington, D.C. Each volunteer worked 20 hours per month and put together 10 reports per month. After the data was compiled in total, 50 people reviewed the data and worked from January 2012 to December 2012.

13. How many reports were generated from February 2010 to April 2010 in Illinois and Ohio?
    A. 3,000   B. 6,000   C. 12,000   D. 15,000   13._____

14. How many volunteers in total collected population data in January 2012?
    A. 10,000   B. 2,000   C. 225   D. 200   14._____

15. How many reports were put together in May 2012?
    A. 2,000   B. 50,000   C. 100,000   D. 100,250   15._____

16. How many hours did the Puerto Rican volunteers work in the fall (September-November)?
    A. 60   B. 500   C. 1,500   D. 0   16._____

17. How many workers were compiling or reviewing data in July 2012?
    A. 25   B. 50   C. 200   D. 250   17._____

18. What was the total amount of hours worked by Nevada volunteers in July 2010?
    A. 500   B. 4,000   C. 4,500   D. 5,000   18._____

19. How many reviewers worked in January 2013?
    A. 75   B. 50   C. 0   D. 25   19._____

20. John has to file 10 documents per shelf. How many documents would it take for John to fill 40 shelves?
    A. 40   B. 400   C. 4,500   D. 5,000   20._____

21. Jill wants to travel from New York City to Los Angeles by bike, which is approximately 2,772 miles. How many miles per day would Jill need to average if she wanted to complete the trip in 4 weeks?
    A. 100   B. 89   C. 99   D. 94   21._____

4 (#2)

22. If there are 24 CPU's and only 7 monitors, how many more monitors do you need to have the same amount of monitors as CPU's?
    A. Not enough information
    B. 17
    C. 31
    D. 0

    22.____

23. If Gerry works 5 days a week and 8 hours each day, and John works 3 days a week and 10 hours each day, how many more hours per year will Gerry work than John?
    A. They work the same amount of hours.
    B. 450
    C. 520
    D. 832

    23.____

24. Jimmy gets transferred to a new office. The new office has 25 employees, but only 16 are there due to a blizzard. How many coworkers was Jimmy able to meet on his first day?
    A. 16
    B. 25
    C. 9
    D. 7

    24.____

25. If you do a fundraiser for charities in your area and raise $500 total, how much would you give to each charity if you were donating equal amounts to 3 of them?
    A. $250.00
    B. $167.77
    C. $50.00
    D. $111.11

    25.____

KEY (CORRECT ANSWERS)

1.	D	11.	C
2.	B	12.	B
3.	A	13.	C
4.	C	14.	A
5.	D	15.	C
6.	B	16.	C
7.	D	17.	B
8.	A	18.	B
9.	A	19.	C
10.	D	20.	B

21. C
22. B
23. C
24. A
25. B

TEST 3

DIRECTIONS: Each question or incomplete statement is followed by several suggested answers or completions. Select the one that BEST answers the question or completes the statement. *PRINT THE LETTER OF THE CORRECT ANSWER IN THE SPACE AT THE RIGHT.*

Questions 1-3.

DIRECTIONS: In answering Questions 1 through 3, choose the correctly spelled word.

1. A. allusion B. alusion C. allusien D. allution 1.____

2. A. altitude B. alltitude C. atlitude D. altlitude 2.____

3. A. althogh B. allthough C. althrough D. although 3.____

Questions 4-9.

DIRECTIONS: In answering Questions 4 through 9, choose the answer that BEST completes the analogy.

4. Odometer is to mileage as compass is to 4.____
   A. speed B. needle C. hiking D. direction

5. Marathon is to race as hibernation is to 5.____
   A. winter B. dream C. sleep D. bear

6. Cup is to coffee as bowl is to 6.____
   A. dish B. spoon C. food D. soup

7. Flow is to river as stagnant is to 7.____
   A. pool B. rain C. stream D. canal

8. Paw is to cat as hoof is to 8.____
   A. lamb B. horse C. lion D. elephant

9. Architect is to building as sculptor is to 9.____
   A. museum B. chisel C. stone D. statue

Questions 10-14.

DIRECTIONS: Questions 10 through 14 are to be answered on the basis of the following graph.

Population of Carroll City Broken Down by Age and Gender (in Thousands)			
Age	Female	Male	Total
Under 15	60	60	120
15-23		22	
24-33		20	44
34-43	13	18	31
44-53	20		67
64 and Over	65	65	130
TOTAL	230	232	462

10. How many people in the city are between the ages of 15-23?
    A. 70 B. 46,000 C. 70,000 D. 225,000

11. Approximately what percentage of the total population of the city was female aged 24-33?
    A. 10% B. 5% C. 15% D. 25%

12. If 33% of the males have a job and 55% of females don't have a job, which of the following statements is TRUE?
    A. Males have approximately 2,600 more jobs than females.
    B. Females have approximately 49,000 more jobs than males.
    C. Females have approximately 26,000 more jobs than males.
    D. None of the above statements are true.

13. How many females between the ages of 15-23 live in Carroll City?
    A. 67,000 B. 24,000 C. 48,000 D. 91,000

14. Assume all males 44-53 living in Carroll City are employed. If two-thirds of males age 44-53 work jobs outside of Carroll City, how many work within city limits?
    A. 31,333
    B. 15,667
    C. 47,000
    D. Cannot answer the question with the information provided

Questions 15-16.

DIRECTIONS: Questions 15 and 16 are labeled as shown. Alphabetize them for filing. Choose the answer that correctly shows the order.

15. (1) AED
    (2) OOS
    (3) FOA
    (4) DOM
    (5) COB

    A. 2-5-4-3-2 B. 1-4-5-2-3 C. 1-5-4-2-3 D. 1-5-4-3-2

15.____

16. Alphabetize the names of the people. Last names are given last.
    (1) Lindsey Jamestown
    (2) Jane Alberta
    (3) Ally Jamestown
    (4) Allison Johnston
    (5) Lyle Moreno

    A. 2-1-3-4-5 B. 3-4-2-1-5 C. 2-3-1-4-5 D. 4-3-2-1-5

16.____

17. Which of the following words is misspelled?
    A. disgust
    B. whisper
    C. locale
    D. none of the above

17.____

Questions 18-21.

DIRECTIONS: Questions 18 through 21 are to be answered on the basis of the following list of employees.

Robertson, Aaron
Bacon, Gina
Jerimiah, Trace
Gillette, Stanley
Jacks, Sharon

18. Which employee name would come in third in alphabetized list?
    A. Robertson, Aaron
    B. Jerimiah, Trace
    C. Gillette, Stanley
    D. Jacks, Sharon

18.____

19. Which employee's first name starts with the letter in the alphabet that is five letters after the first letter of their last name?
    A. Jerimiah, Trace
    B. Bacon, Gina
    C. Jacks, Sharon
    D. Gillette, Stanley

19.____

20. How many employees have last names that are exactly five letters long?
    A. 1 B. 2 C. 3 D. 4

20.____

21. How many of the employees have either a first or last name that starts with the letter "G"?
    A. 1   B. 2   C. 4   D. 5

Questions 22-25.

DIRECTIONS: Questions 22 through 25 are to be answered on the basis of the following chart.

Bicycle Sales (Model #34JA32)							
Country	May	June	July	August	September	October	Total
Germany	34	47	45	54	56	60	296
Britain	40	44	36	47	47	46	260
Ireland	37	32	32	32	34	33	200
Portugal	14	14	14	16	17	14	89
Italy	29	29	28	31	29	31	177
Belgium	22	24	24	26	25	23	144
Total	176	198	179	206	208	207	1166

22. What percentage of the overall total was sold to the German importer?
    A. 25.3%   B. 22%   C. 24.1%   D. 23%

23. What percentage of the overall total was sold in September?
    A. 24.1%   B. 25.6%   C. 17.9%   D. 24.6%

24. What is the average number of units per month imported into Belgium over the first four months shown?
    A. 26   B. 20   C. 24   D. 31

25. If you look at the three smallest importers, what is their total import percentage?
    A. 35.1%   B. 37.1%   C. 40%   D. 28%

KEY (CORRECT ANSWERS)

1. A
2. A
3. D
4. D
5. C

6. D
7. A
8. B
9. D
10. C

11. B
12. C
13. C
14. B
15. D

16. C
17. D
18. D
19. B
20. B

21. B
22. A
23. C
24. C
25. A

TEST 4

DIRECTIONS: Each question or incomplete statement is followed by several suggested answers or completions. Select the one that BEST answers the question or completes the statement. *PRINT THE LETTER OF THE CORRECT ANSWER IN THE SPACE AT THE RIGHT.*

Questions 1-6.

DIRECTIONS: In answering Questions 1 through 6, choose the sentence that represents the BEST example of English grammar.

1. A. Joey and me want to go on a vacation next week.   1.____
    B. Gary told Jim he would need to take some time off.
    C. If turning six years old, Jim's uncle would teach Spanish to him.
    D. Fax a copy of your resume to Ms. Perez and me.

2. A. Jerry stood in line for almost two hours.   2.____
    B. The reaction to my engagement was less exciting than I thought it would be.
    C. Carlos and me have done great work on this project.
    D. Two parts of the speech needs to be revised before tomorrow.

3. A. Arriving home, the alarm was tripped.   3.____
    B. Jonny is regarded as a stand up guy, a responsible parent, and he doesn't give up until a task is finished.
    C. Each employee must submit a drug test each month.
    D. One of the documents was incinerated in the explosion.

4. A. As soon as my parents get home, I told them I finished all of my chores.   4.____
    B. I asked my teacher to send me my missing work, check my absences, and how did I do on my test.
    C. Matt attempted to keep it concealed from Jenny and me.
    D. If Mary or him cannot get work done on time, I will have to split them up.

5. A. Driving to work, the traffic report warned him of an accident on Highway 47.   5.____
    B. Jimmy has performed well this season.
    C. Since finishing her degree, several job offers have been given to Cam.
    D. Our boss is creating unstable conditions for we employees.

6. A. The thief was described as a tall man with a wiry mustache weighing approximately 150 pounds.   6.____
    B. She gave Patrick and I some more time to finish our work.
    C. One of the books that he ordered was damaged in shipping.
    D. While talking on the rotary phone, the car Jim was driving skidded off the road.

Questions 7-9.

DIRECTIONS: Questions 7 through 9 are to be answered on the basis of the following graph.

Ice Lake Frozen Flight (2002-2013)		
Year	Number of Participants	Temperature (Fahrenheit)
2002	22	4°
2003	50	33°
2004	69	18°
2005	104	22°
2006	108	24°
2007	288	33°
2008	173	9°
2009	598	39°
2010	698	26°
2011	696	30°
2012	777	28°
2013	578	32°

7. Which two year span had the LARGEST difference between temperatures?
   A. 2002 and 2003
   B. 2011 and 2012
   C. 2008 and 2009
   D. 2003 and 2004

7.____

8. How many total people participated in the years after the temperature reached at least 29°?
   A. 2,295
   B. 1,717
   C. 2,210
   D. 4,543

8.____

9. In 2007, the event saw 288 participants, while in 2008 that number dropped to 173. Which of the following reasons BEST explains the drop in participants?
   A. The event had not been going on that long and people didn't know about it.
   B. The lake water wasn't cold enough to have people jump in.
   C. The temperature was too cold for many people who would have normally participated.
   D. None of the above reasons explain the drop in participants.

9.____

10. In the following list of numbers, how many times does 4 come just after 2 when 2 comes just after an odd number?
    2365247653898632488572486392424
    A. 2
    B. 3
    C. 4
    D. 5

10.____

11. Which choice below lists the letter that is as far after B as S is after N in the alphabet?
    A. G
    B. H
    C. I
    D. J

11.____

Questions 12-15.

DIRECTIONS: Questions 12 through 15 are to be answered on the basis of the following directory and list of changes.

Directory		
Name	Emp. Type	Position
Julie Taylor	Warehouse	Packer
James King	Office	Administrative Assistant
John Williams	Office	Salesperson
Ray Moore	Warehouse	Maintenance
Kathleen Byrne	Warehouse	Supervisor
Amy Jones	Office	Salesperson
Paul Jonas	Office	Salesperson
Lisa Wong	Warehouse	Loader
Eugene Lee	Office	Accountant
Bruce Lavine	Office	Manager
Adam Gates	Warehouse	Packer
Will Suter	Warehouse	Packer
Gary Lorper	Office	Accountant
Jon Adams	Office	Salesperson
Susannah Harper	Office	Salesperson

Directory Updates:
- Employee e-mail addresses will adhere to the following guidelines: lastnamefirstname@apexindustries.com (ex. Susannah Harper is harpersusannah@apexindustries.com). Currently, employees in the warehouse share one e-mail, distribution@apexindustries.com.
- The "Loader" position will now be referred to as "Specialist I"
- Adam Gates has accepted a Supervisor position within the Warehouse and is no longer a Packer. All warehouse employees report to the two Supervisors and all office employees report to the Manager.

12. Amy Jones tried to send an e-mail to Adam Gates, but it wouldn't send.   12.____
    Which of the following offers the BEST explanation?
    A. Amy put Adam's first name first and then his last name.
    B. Adam doesn't check his e-mail, so he wouldn't know if he received the e-mail or not.
    C. Adam does not have his own e-mail.
    D. Office employees are not allowed to send e-mails to each other.

13. How many Packers currently work for Apex Industries?   13.____
    A. 2   B. 3   C. 4   D. 5

14. What position does Lisa Wong currently hold?   14.____
    A. Specialist I   B. Secretary
    C. Administrative Assistant   D. Loader

15. If an employee wanted to contact the office manager, which of the following e-mails should the e-mail be sent to?
    A. officemanager@apexindustries.com
    B. brucelavine@apexindustries.com
    C. lavinebruce@apexindustries.com
    D. distribution@apexindustries.com

15._____

Questions 16-19.

DIRECTIONS: In answering Questions 16 through 19, compare the three names, numbers or addresses.

16. Smiley Yarnell   Smiley Yarnel   Smily Yarnell
    A. All three are exactly alike.
    B. The first and second are exactly alike.
    C. The second and third are exactly alike.
    D. All three are different.

16._____

17. 1583 Theater Drive   1583 Theater Drive   1583 Theatre Drive
    A. All three are exactly alike.
    B. The first and second are exactly alike.
    C. The second and third are exactly alike.
    D. All three are different.

17._____

18. 3341893212   3341893212   3341893212
    A. All three are exactly alike.
    B. The first and second are exactly alike.
    C. The second and third are exactly alike.
    D. All three are different.

18._____

19. Douglass Watkins   Douglas Watkins   Douglass Watkins
    A. All three are exactly alike.
    B. The first and third are exactly alike.
    C. The second and third are exactly alike.
    D. All three are different.

19._____

Questions 20-24.

DIRECTIONS: In answering Questions 20 through 24, you will be presented with a word. Choose the synonym that BEST represents the word in question.

20. Flexible
    A. delicate   B. inflammable   C. strong   D. pliable

20._____

21. Alternative
    A. choice   B. moderate   C. lazy   D. value

21._____

22. Corroborate
    A. examine   B. explain   C. verify   D. explain

23. Respiration
    A. recovery   B. breathing   C. sweating   D. selfish

24. Negligent
    A. lazy   B. moderate   C. hopeless   D. lax

25. Plumber is to Wrench as Painter is to
    A. pipe   B. shop   C. hammer   D. brush

22.____
23.____
24.____
25.____

KEY (CORRECT ANSWERS)

1.	D	11.	A
2.	A	12.	C
3.	D	13.	A
4.	C	14.	A
5.	B	15.	C
6.	C	16.	D
7.	C	17.	B
8.	B	18.	A
9.	C	19.	B
10.	C	20.	D

21. A
22. C
23. B
24. D
25. D

NAME AND NUMBER CHECKING
EXAMINATION SECTION
TEST 1

DIRECTIONS: This test is designed to measure your speed/and accuracy. You are urged to work both quickly and accurately and to do correctly as many lists as you can in the time allowed. The test consists of lists or pairs of names and numbers. Count the number of IDENTICAL pairs in each list. Then, select the correct number, 1, 2, 3, 4, 5, and indicate your choice in the space at the right. Two sample questions are presented for your guidance, together with the correct solutions.

<u>SAMPLE LIST A</u>
Adelphi College – Adelphia College
Braxton Corp – Braxeton Corp.
Wassaic State School – Wassaic State School
Central Islip State Hospital – Central Isllip State Hospital
Greenwich House – Greenwich House

NOTE: There are only two correct pairs—Wassaic State School and Greenwich House. Therefore, the CORRECT answer is 2.

<u>SAMPLE LIST B</u>
78453694 – 78453684
784530 – 784530
533 – 534
67845 – 67845
2368745 – 2368755

NOTE: There are only two correct pairs—784530 and 67845. Therefore, the CORRECT answer is 2.

<u>LIST 1</u>   1._____
    Diagnostic Clinic   – Diagnostic Clinic
    Yorkville Health   – Yorkville Health
    Meinhard Clinic   – Meinhart Clinic
    Corlears Clinic   – Carlears Clinic
    Tremont Diagnostic   – Tremont Diagnostic

<u>LIST 2</u>   2._____
    73526   – 73526
    7283627198   – 7283627198
    627   – 637
    728352617283   – 7283526178282
    6281   – 6281

2 (#1)

LIST 3   3.____
    Jefferson Clinic   – Jeffersen Clinic
    Mott Haven Center   – Mott Havan Center
    Bronx Hospital   – Bronx Hospital
    Montefiore Hospital   – Montifeore Hospital
    Beth Isreal Hospital   – Beth Israel Hospital

LIST 4   4.____
    936271826   – 936371826
    5271   – 5291
    82637192037   – 82637192037
    527182   – 5271882
    726354256   - 72635456

LIST 5   5.____
    Trinity Hospital   – Trinity Hospital
    Central Harlem   – Centrel Harlem
    St. Luke's Hospital   – St. Lukes' Hospital
    Mt. Sinai Hospital   – Mt. Sinia Hospital
    N.Y. Dispensery   – N.Y. Dispensary

LIST 6   6.____
    725361552637   – 725361555637
    7526378   – 7526377
    6975   – 6975
    82637481028   – 82637481028
    3427   – 3429

LIST 7   7.____
    Misericordia Hospital – Miseracordia Hospital
    Lebonan Hospital   – Lebanon Hospital
    Gouverneur Hospital – Gouverner Hospital
    German Polyclinic   – German Policlinic
    French Hospital   – French Hospital

LIST 8   8.____
    8277364933251   – 827364933351
    63728   – 63728
    367281   – 367281
    62733846273   – 6273846293
    62836   - 6283

LIST 9   9.____
    King's County Hospital – Kings County Hospital
    St. Johns Long Island – St. John's Long Island
    Bellevue Hospital   – Bellvue Hospital
    Beth David Hospital – Beth David Hospital
    Samaritan Hospital   – Samariton Hospital

3 (#1)

LIST 10   10.____
    62836454   – 62836455
    42738267   – 42738369
    573829   – 573829
    738291627874   – 738291627874
    725   - 735

LIST 11   11.____
    Bloomingdal Clinic   – Bloomingdale Clinic
    Communitty Hospital   – Community Hospital
    Metroplitan Hospital   – Metropoliton Hospital
    Lenox Hill Hospital   – Lonex Hill Hospital
    Lincoln Hospital   – Lincoln Hospital

LIST 12   12.____
    6283364728   – 6283648
    627385   – 627383
    54283902   – 54283602
    63354   – 63354
    7283562781   - 7283562781

LIST 13   13.____
    Sydenham Hospital   – Sydanham Hospital
    Roosevalt Hospital   – Roosevelt Hospital
    Vanderbilt Clinic   – Vanderbild Clinic
    Women's Hospital   – Woman's Hospital
    Flushing Hospital   – Flushing Hospital

LIST 14   14.____
    62738   – 62738
    727355542321   – 72735542321
    263849332   – 263849332
    262837   – 263837
    47382912   - 47382922

LIST 15   15.____
    Episcopal Hospital   – Episcapal Hospital
    Flower Hospital   – Flouer Hospital
    Stuyvesent Clinic   – Stuyvesant Clinic
    Jamaica Clinic   – Jamaica Clinic
    Ridgwood Clinic   – Ridgewood Clinic

LIST 16   16.____
    628367299   – 628367399
    111   – 111
    118293304829   – 1182839489
    4448   – 4448
    333693678   - 333693678

4 (#1)

LIST 17   17.____
    Arietta Crane Farm   – Areitta Crane Farm
    Bikur Chilim Home   – Bikur Chilom Home
    Burke Foundation   – Burke Foundation
    Blythedale Home   – Blythdale Home
    Campbell Cottages   – Cambell Cottages

LIST 18   18.____
    32123   – 32132
    273893326783   – 27389326783
    473829   – 473829
    7382937   – 7383937
    3628890122332   - 36289012332

LIST 19   19.____
    Caraline Rest   – Caroline Rest
    Loreto Rest   – Loretto Rest
    Edgewater Creche   – Edgwater Creche
    Holiday Farm   – Holiday Farm
    House of St. Giles   – House of st. Giles

LIST 20   20.____
    557286777   – 55728677
    3678902   – 3678892
    1567839   – 1567839
    7865434712   – 7865344712
    9927382   - 9927382

LIST 21   21.____
    Isabella Home   – Isabela Home
    James A. Moore Home   – James A. More Home
    The Robin's Nest   – The Roben's Nest
    Pelham Home   – Pelam Home
    St. Eleanora's Home   – St. Eleanora's Home

LIST 22   22.____
    273648293048   – 273648293048
    334   – 334
    7362536478   – 7362536478
    7362819273   – 7362819273
    7362   - 7363

LIST 23   23.____
    St. Pheobe's Mission   – St. Phebe's Mission
    Seaside Home   – Seaside Home
    Speedwell Society   – Speedwell Society
    Valeria Home   – Valera Home
    Wiltwyck   - Wildwyck

5 (#1)

LIST 24
    63728   – 63738
    63728192736   – 63728192738
    428   – 458
    62738291527   – 62738291529
    63728192   - 63728192

24.____

LIST 25
    McGaffin   – McGafin
    David Ardslee   – David Ardslee
    Axton Supply   – Axeton Supply Co
    Alice Russell   – Alice Russell
    Dobson Mfg. Co. – Dobsen Mfg. Co.

25.____

KEY (CORRECT ANSWERS)

1.	3		11.	1
2.	3		12.	2
3.	1		13.	1
4.	1		14.	2
5.	1		15.	1
6.	2		16.	3
7.	1		17.	1
8.	2		18.	1
9.	1		19.	1
10.	2		20.	2

        21.   1
        22.   4
        23.   2
        24.   1
        25.   2

TEST 2

DIRECTIONS: This test is designed to measure your speed/and accuracy. You are urged to work both quickly and accurately and to do correctly as many lists as you can in the time allowed. The test consists of lists or pairs of names and numbers. Count the number of IDENTICAL pairs in each list. Then, select the correct number, 1, 2, 3, 4, 5, and indicate your choice in the space at the right.

LIST 1   1.____
   82637381028   – 82637281028
   928   – 928
   72937281028   – 72937281028
   7362   – 7362
   927382615   – 927382615

LIST 2   2.____
   Albee Theatre   – Albee Theatre
   Lapland Lumber Co.   – Laplund Lumber Co.
   Adelphi College   – Adelphi College
   Jones & Son Inc.   – Jones & Sons Inc.
   S.W. Ponds Co.   – S.W. Ponds Co.

LIST 3   3.____
   85345   – 85345
   895643278   – 895643277
   726352   – 726353
   632685   – 632685
   7263524   – 7236524

LIST 4   4.____
   Eagle Library   – Eagle Library
   Dodge Ltd.   – Dodge Co.
   Stromberg Carlson   – Stromberg Carlsen
   Clairice Ling   – Clairice Linng
   Mason Book Co.   – Matson Book Co.

LIST 5   5.____
   66273   – 66273
   629   – 629
   7382517283   – 7382517283
   637281   – 639281
   2738261   – 2788261

LIST 6   6.____
   Robert MacColl   – Robert McColl
   Buick Motor   – Buck Motors
   Murray Bay & Co. Ltd.   – Murray Bay Co. Ltd.
   L.T. Ltyle   – L.T. Lyttle
   A.S. Landas   – A.S. Landas

2 (#2)

LIST 7
    6271526374890   – 627152637490
    73526189   – 73526189
    5372   – 5392
    637281142   – 63728124
    4783946   – 4783046

7.____

LIST 8
    Tyndall Burke   – Tyndell Burke
    W. Briehl   – W. Briehl
    Burritt Publishing Co.   – Buritt Publishing Co.
    Frederick Breyer & Co.   – Frederick Breyer Co.
    Bailey Buulard   – Bailey Bullard

8.____

LIST 9
    634   – 634
    16837   – 163837
    273892223678   – 27389223678
    527182   – 527782
    3628901223   – 3629002223

9.____

LIST 10
    Ernest Boas   – Ernest Boas
    Rankin Barne   – Rankin Barnes
    Edward Appley   – Edward Appely
    Camel   – Camel
    Caiger Food Co.   – Caiger Food Co.

10.____

LIST 11
    6273   – 6273
    322   – 332
    15672839   – 15672839
    63728192637   – 63728192639
    738   – 738

11.____

LIST 12
    Wells Fargo Co.   – Wells Fargo Co.
    W.D. Brett   – W.D. Britt
    Tassco Co.   – Tassko Co.
    Republic Mills   – Republic Mill
    R.W. Burnham   – R.W. Burhnam

12.____

LIST 13
    7253529152   – 7283529152
    6283   – 6383
    52839102738   – 5283910238
    308   – 398
    82637201927   – 8263720127

13.____

LIST 14
    Schumacker Co.   – Shumacker Co.
    C.H. Caiger   – C.H. Caiger
    Abraham Strauss   – Abram Straus
    B.F. Boettjer   – B.F. Boettijer
    Cut-Rate Store   – Cut-Rate Stores

14.____

LIST 15
    15273826   – 15273826
    72537   – 73537
    726391027384   – 62639107384
    637389   – 627399
    725382910   – 725382910

15.____

LIST 16
    Hixby Ltd.   – Hixby Lt'd.
    S. Reiner   – S. Riener
    Reynard Co.   – Reynord Co.
    Esso Gassoline Co.   – Esso Gasolene Co.
    Belle Brock   – Belle Brock

16.____

LIST 17
    7245   – 7245
    819263728192   – 819263728172
    682537289   – 682537298
    789   – 789
    82936542891   – 82936542891

17.____

LIST 18
    Joseph Cartwright   – Joseph Cartwrite
    Foote Food Co.   – Foot Food Co.
    Weiman & Held   – Weiman & Held
    Sanderson Shoe Co.   – Sandersen Shoe Co.
    A.M. Byrne   – A.N. Byrne

18.____

LIST 19
    4738267   – 4738277
    63728   – 63729
    6283628901   – 6283628991
    918264   – 918264
    263728192037   – 2637728192073

19.____

LIST 20
    Exray Laboratories   – Exray Labratories
    Curley Toy Co.   – Curly Toy Co.
    J. Lauer & Cross   – J. Laeur & Cross
    Mireco Brands   – Mireco Brands
    Sandor Lorand   – Sandor Larand

20.____

4 (#2)

LIST 21   21.____
   607   – 609
   6405   – 6403
   976   – 996
   101267   – 101267
   2065432   – 20965432

LIST 22   22.____
   John Macy & Sons   – John Macy & Son
   Venus Pencil Co.   – Venus Pencil Co.
   Nell McGinnis   – Nell McGinnis
   McCutcheon & Co.   – McCutcheon & Co.
   Sun-Tan Oil   – Sun-Tan Oil

LIST 23   23.____
   703345700   – 703345700
   46754   – 466754
   3367490   – 3367490
   3379   – 3778
   47384   – 47394

LIST 24   24.____
   arthritis   – arthritis
   asthma   – asthma
   endocrine   – endocrene
   gastro-enterological   – gastrol-enteralogical
   orthopedic   – orthopedic

LIST 25   25.____
   743829432   – 743828432
   998   – 998
   732816253902   – 732816252902
   46829   – 46830
   7439120249   – 7439210249

KEY (CORRECT ANSWERS)

1.	4	11.	3
2.	3	12.	1
3.	2	13.	1
4.	1	14.	1
5.	2	15.	2
6.	1	16.	1
7.	2	17.	3
8.	1	18.	1
9.	1	19.	1
10.	3	20.	1

21.	1
22.	4
23.	2
24.	3
25.	1

ADDRESS CHECKING

EXAMINATION SECTION
TEST 1

DIRECTIONS: This test is designed to measure your speed and accuracy. You are urged to work both quickly and accurately and to do correctly as many lists as you can in the time allowed. The test consists of lists of pairs of addresses. Circle the letter *A* on your answer sheet if the two addresses are exactly ALIKE in every way. Circle the letter *D* if they are DIFFERENT.

CIRCLE CORRECT ANSWER

1.	405 Winter Rd NW	405 Winter Rd NW	A	D
2.	607 S Calaveras Rd	607 S Calaveras Rd	A	D
3.	8406 La Casa St	8406 La Cosa St	A	D
4.	121 N Rippon St	121 N Rippon St	A	D
5.	Wideman Ar	Wiseman Ar	A	D
6.	Sodus NY 14551	Sodus NY 14551	A	D
7.	3429 Hermosa Dr	3429 Hermoso Dr	A	D
8.	3628 S Zeeland St	3268 S Zeeland St	A	D
9.	1330 Cheverly Ave NE	1330 Cheverly Ave NE	A	D
10.	1689 N Derwood Dr	1689 N Derwood Dr	A	D
11.	3886 Sunrise Ct	3886 Sunrise Ct	A	D
12.	635 La Calle Mayor	653 La Calle Mayor	A	D
13.	2560 Lansford Pl	2560 Lansford St	A	D
14.	4631 Central Ave	4631 Central Ave	A	D
15.	Mason City Ia 50401	Mason City Ia 50401	A	D
16.	758 Los Arboles Ave SE	758 Los Arboles Ave SW	A	D
17.	3282 E Downington St	3282 E Dunnington St	A	D
18.	7117 N Burlingham Ave	7117 N Burlingham Ave	A	D
19.	32 Oaklawn Blvd	32 Oakland Blvd	A	D
20.	1274 Manzana Rd	1274 Manzana Rd	A	D

KEY (CORRECT ANSWERS)

1. A	6. A	11. A	16. D
2. A	7. D	12. D	17. D
3. D	8. D	13. D	18. A
4. A	9. A	14. A	19. D
5. D	10. A	15. A	20. A

TEST 2

DIRECTIONS: This test is designed to measure your speed and accuracy. You are urged to work both quickly and accurately and to do correctly as many lists as you can in the time allowed. The test consists of lists of pairs of addresses. Circle the letter A on your answer sheet if the two addresses are exactly ALIKE in every way. Circle the letter D if they are DIFFERENT.

			CIRCLE CORRECT ANSWER	
1.	4598 E Kenilworth Dr	4598 E Kenilworth Dr	A	D
2.	Dayton Ok 73449	Dagton Ok 73449	A	D
3.	1172 W 83rd Ave	1127 W 83rd Ave	A	D
4.	6434 E Pulaski St	6434 E Pulaski Ct	A	D
5.	2764 N Rutherford Pl	2764 N Rutherford Pl	A	D
6.	565 Greenville Blvd SW	565 Greenview Blvd SE	A	D
7.	3824 Massasoit St	3824 Massasoit St	A	D
8.	22 Sagnaw Pkwy	22 Saganaw Pkwy	A	D
9.	Byram Ct 10573	Byram Ct 10573	A	D
10.	1928 S Fairfield Ave	1928 S Fairfield St	A	D
11.	36218 Overhills Dr	36218 Overhills Dr	A	D
13.	516 Avenida de Las Americas NW	516 Avenida de Las Americas NW	A	D
14.	7526 Naraganset Pl SW	7526 Naraganset Pl SW	A	D
15.	52626 W Ogelsby Dr	52626 W Ogelsby Dr	A	D
16.	1003 Winchester Rd	1003 Westchester Rd	A	D
17.	3478 W Cavanaugh Ct	3478 W Cavenaugh Ct	A	D
18.	Kendall Ca 90551	Kendell Ca 90551	A	D
19.	225 El Camino Blvd	225 El Camino Av	A	D
20.	7310 Via de los Pisos	7310 Via de los Pinos	A	D

KEY (CORRECT ANSWERS)

1. A	6. D	11. D	16. D
2. D	7. D	12. A	17. D
3. D	8. A	13. A	18. D
4. D	9. D	14. A	19. D
5. A	10. A	15. A	20. D

———

TEST 3

DIRECTIONS: This test is designed to measure your speed and accuracy. You are urged to work both quickly and accurately and to do correctly as many lists as you can in the time allowed. The test consists of lists of pairs of addresses. Circle the letter *A* on your answer sheet if the two addresses are exactly ALIKE in every way. Circle the letter *D* if they are DIFFERENT.

			CIRCLE CORRECT ANSWER	
1.	1987 Wellington Ave SW	1987 Wellington Ave SW	A	D
2.	3124 S 71st St	3142 S 71st St	A	D
3.	729 Lincolnwood Blvd	729 Lincolnwood Blvd	A	D
4.	1166 N Beaumont Dr	1166 S Beaumont Dr	A	D
5.	3224 W Winecona Pl	3224 W Winecona Pl	A	D
6.	608 La Calle Bienvenida	607 La Calle Bienvenida	A	D
7.	La Molte Ia 52045	La Molte Ia 52045	A	D
8.	8625 Armitage Ave NW	8625 Armitage Ave NW	A	D
9.	2343 Broadview Ave	2334 Broadview Ave	A	D
10.	4279 Sierra Grande -Ave NE	427-9 Sierra Grande Dr NE	A	D
11.	165 32d Ave	165 32d Ave	A	D
12.	12742 N Deerborn St	12724 N Deerborn St	A	D
13.	114 Estancia Ave	141 Estancia Ave	A	D
14.	351 S Berwyn Rd	351 S Berwyn Pl	A	D
15.	7732 Avenida Manana SW	7732 Avenida Manana SW	A	D
16.	6337 C St SW	6337 G St SW	A	D
17.	57895 E Drexyl Ave	58795 E Drexyl Ave	A	D
18.	Altro Tx 75923	Altra Tx 75923	A	D
19.	3465 S Nashville St	3465 N Nashville St	A	D
20.	1226 Odell Blvd NW	1226 Oddell Blvd NW	A	D

KEY (CORRECT ANSWERS)

1. A	6. D	11. A	16. D
2. D	7. A	12. D	17. D
3. A	8. A	13. D	18. D
4. D	9. D	14. D	19. D
5. A	10. D	15. A	20. D

TEST 4

DIRECTIONS: This test is designed to measure your speed and accuracy. You are urged to work both quickly and accurately and to do correctly as many lists as you can in the time allowed. The test consists of lists of pairs of addresses. Circle the letter A on your answer sheet if the two addresses are exactly ALIKE in every way. Circle the letter D if they are DIFFERENT.

CIRCLE
CORRECT ANSWER

1. 94002 Chappel Ct   94002 Chappel Ct   A   D
2. 512 La Vega Dr   512 La Veta Dr   A   D
3. 8774 W Winona Pl   8774 E Winona Pl   A   D
4. 6431 Ingleside St SE   6431 Ingleside St SE   A   D
5. 2270 N Leanington St   2270 N Leanington St   A   D
6. 235 Calle de Los Vecinos   235 Calle de Los Vecinos   A   D
7. 3987 E Westwood Ave   3987 W Westwood Ave   A   D
8. Skamokawa Wa   Skamohawa Wa   A   D
9. 2674 E Champlain Cir   2764 E Champlain Cir   A   D
10. 8751 Elmhurst Blvd   8751 Elmwood Blvd   A   D
11. 6649 Solano Dr   6649 Solana Dr   A   D
12. 4423 S Escenaba St   4423 S Escenaba St   A   D
13. 1198 N St NW   1198 M St NW   A   D
14. Sparta Ga   Sparta Va   A   D
15. 96753 Wrightwood Ave   96753 Wrightwood Ave   A   D
16. 2445 Sangamow Ave SE   2445 Sangamow Ave SE   A   D
17. 5117 E 67 Pl   5171 E 67 Pl   A   D
18. 847 Mesa Grande Pl   847 Mesa Grande Ct   A   D
19. 1100 Cermaken St   1100 Cermaker St   A   D
20. 321 Tijeras Ave NW   321 Tijeras Ave NW   A   D

KEY (CORRECT ANSWERS)

1. A	6. A	11. D	16. A
2. D	7. D	12. A	17. D
3. D	8. D	13. D	18. D
4. A	9. D	14. D	19. D
5. A	10. D	15. A	20. A

TEST 5

DIRECTIONS: This test is designed to measure your speed and accuracy. You are urged to work both quickly and accurately and to do correctly as many lists as you can in the time allowed. The test consists of lists of pairs of addresses. Circle the letter *A* on your answer sheet if the two addresses are exactly ALIKE in every way. Circle the letter *D* if they are DIFFERENT.

CIRCLE CORRECT ANSWER

#	Address 1	Address 2	A	D
1.	3405 Prospect St	3405 Prospect St	A	D
2.	6643 Burlington Pl	6643 Burlingtown Pl	A	D
3.	851 Esperanza Blvd	851 Esperanza Blvd	A	D
4.	Jenkinjones WV	Kenkinjones W	A	D
5.	1008 Pennsylvania Ave SE	1008 Pennsylvania Ave SW	A	D
6.	2924 26th St N	2929 26th St N	A	D
7.	7115 Highland Dr	7115 Highland Dr	A	D
8.	Chaptico Md	Chaptica Md	A	D
9.	3508 Camron Mills Rd	3508 Camron Mills Rd	A	D
10.	67158 Capston Dr	67158 Capston Dr	A	D
11.	3613 S Taylor Av	3631 S Taylor Av	A	D
12.	2421 Menokin Dr	2421 Menokin Dr	A	D
13.	3226 M St NW	3226 N St NW	A	D
14.	1201 S Court House Rd	1201 S Court House Rd	A	D
15.	Findlay Ohio 45840	Findley Ohio 45840	A	D
16.	17 Bennett St	17 Bennet St	A	D
17.	7 Vine Bowl Dr	7 Vine Bowl Pl	A	D
18.	126 McKinley Av	126 MacKinley Av	A	D
19.	384 Nepperhan Rd	387 Nepperhan Rd	A	D
20.	1077 Contreras Av NW	1077 Contreras Av NW	A	D

KEY (CORRECT ANSWERS)

1.	A	6.	D	11.	D	16.	D
2.	D	7.	A	12.	A	17.	D
3.	A	8.	D	13.	D	18.	D
4.	D	9.	A	14.	A	19.	D
5.	D	10.	A	15.	D	20.	A

TEST 6

DIRECTIONS: This test is designed to measure your speed and accuracy. You are urged to work both quickly and accurately and to do correctly as many lists as you can in the time allowed. The test consists of lists of pairs of addresses. Circle the letter A on your answer sheet if the two addresses are exactly ALIKE in every way. Circle the letter D if they are DIFFERENT.

CIRCLE
CORRECT ANSWER

1.	239 Summit Pl NE	239 Summit Pl NE	A	D
2.	152 Continental Pkwy	152 Continental Blvd	A	D
3.	8092 13th Rd S	8029 13th Rd S	A	D
4.	3906 Queensbury Rd	3906 Queensbury Rd	A	D
5.	4719 Linnean Av NW	4719 Linnean Av NE	A	D
6.	Bradford Me	Bradley Me	A	D
7.	Parrott Ga 31777	Parrott Ga 31177	A	D
8.	4312 Lowell Lane	4312 Lowell Lane	A	D
9.	6929 W 135th Place	6929 W 135th Plaza	A	D
10.	5143 Somerset Cir	5143 Somerset Cir	A	D
11.	8501 Kennedy St	8501 Kennedy St	A	D
12.	2164 E McLean Av	2164 E McLean Av	A	D
13.	7186 E St NW	7186 F St NW	A	D
14.	2121 Beechcrest Rd	2121 Beechcroft Rd	A	D
15.	324 S Alvadero St	324 S Alverado St	A	D
17.	2908 Plaza de las Estrellas	2908 Plaza de las Estrellas	A	D
18.	223 Great Falls Rd SE	223 Great Falls Dr SE	A	D
19.	Kelton SC 29354	Kelton SC 29354	A	D
20.	3201 Landover Rd	3201 Landover Rd	A	D

KEY (CORRECT ANSWERS)

1. A	6. D	11. A	16. D
2. D	7. D	12. A	17. A
3. D	8. A	13. D	18. D
4. A	9. D	14. D	19. A
5. D	10. A	15. A	20. A

TEST 7

DIRECTIONS: This test is designed to measure your speed and accuracy. You are urged to work both quickly and accurately and to do correctly as many lists as you can in the time allowed. The test consists of lists of pairs of addresses. Circle the letter A on your answer sheet if the two addresses are exactly ALIKE in every way. Circle the letter D if they are DIFFERENT.

			CIRCLE CORRECT ANSWER	
1.	111 Caroline Pl Armnk	111 Caroline Pl Armnk	A	D
2.	21 Grnleaf Rye	121 Grnleaf Rye	A	D
3.	245 Rumsy Rd Ynkrs	245 Rumsey Rd Ynkrs	A	D
4.	927 South Peekskl	927 South Pekskl	A	D
5.	44 Monro Av Lrchmt	44 Monroe Av Lrchmt	A	D
6.	39 Andrea Ln Scrsdl	39 Andrea La Scrsdl	A	D
7.	Ruland Wy 62143	Ruland Wy 62143	A	D
8.	51 Cyprs Rd Tukaho	51 Cyprs Rd Tuckaho	A	D
9.	213 Shore Lane Rd Mahopc	213 Shore Lane Av Mahopc	A	D
10.	189 Colmbs Av Lk Oscawna	189 Columbus Av Lk Oscawna	A	D
11.	124 West Stationery Rd	124 West Stationary Rd	A	D
12.	Purdy Vt 03124	Purdy Vt 03124	A	D
13.	129 Tewksbury Rd	129 Twsksbury Rd	A	D
14.	Gallow Hill Rd SW	Gallow Hill Rd	A	D
15.	234 Myrtle Av	234 Myrtl Av	A	D
16.	35 Chase Pl NE	35 Chse Pl NE	A	D
17.	14 Terace Av	41 Terace Av	A	D
18.	Collins Pt Rd SE	Colins Pt Rd SE	A	D
19.	164 Sagmor Ct	164 Sagmor Ct	A	D
20.	117 Warburtn Dr NE	117 Wrburtn Dr NE	A	D

KEY (CORRECT ANSWERS)

1. A	6. D	11. D	16. D
2. D	7. A	12. A	17. D
3. D	8. D	13. D	18. D
4. D	9. D	14. D	19. A
5. D	10. D	15. D	20. D

CODING
EXAMINATION SECTION
COMMENTARY

An ingenious question-type called coding, involving elements of alphabetizing, filing, name and number comparison, and evaluative judgment and application, has currently won wide acceptance in testing circles for measuring clerical aptitude and general ability, particularly on the senior (middle) grades (levels).

While the directions for this question usually vary in detail, the candidate is generally asked to consider groups of names, codes, and numbers, and then, according to a given plan, to arrange codes in alphabetic order; to arrange these in numerical sequence; to re-arrange columns of names and numbers in correct order; to espy errors in coding; to choose the correct coding arrangement in consonance with the given directions and examples, etc.

This question-type appear to have few parameters in respect to form, substance, or degree of difficulty.

Accordingly, acquaintance with, and practice in, the coding question is recommended for the serious candidate.

TEST 1

DIRECTIONS: Questions 1 through 8 are to be answered on the basis of the code table and the instructions given below.

Code Letter for Traffic Problem	B	H	Q	J	F	L	M	I
Code Number for Action Taken	1	2	3	4	5	6	7	8

Assume that each of the capital letters on the above chart is a radio code for a particular traffic problem and that the number immediately below each capital letter is the radio code for the correct action to be taken to deal with the problem. For instance, "1" is the action to be taken to deal with problem "B", "2" is the action to be taken to deal with problem "H", and so forth.

In each question, a series of code letters is given in Column 1. Column 2 gives four different arrangements of code numbers. You are to pick the answer (A, B, C, or D) in Column 2 that gives the code numbers that match the code letters in the same order.

SAMPLE QUESTION

Column 1
BHLFMQ

Column 2
A. 125678
B. 216573
C. 127653
D. 126573

According to the chart, the code numbers that correspond to these code letters are as follows: B – 1, M – 2, L – 6, F – 5, M – 7, Q – 3. Therefore, the right answer is 126573. This answer is D in Column 2.

2 (#1)

	Column 1		Column 2	

1. BHQLMI
   - A. 123456
   - B. 123567
   - C. 123678
   - D. 125678

   1.____

2. HBJQLF
   - A. 214365
   - B. 213456
   - C. 213465
   - D. 214387

   2.____

3. QHMLFJ
   - A. 321654
   - B. 345678
   - C. 327645
   - D. 327654

   3.____

4. FLQJIM
   - A. 543287
   - B. 563487
   - C. 564378
   - D. 654378

   4.____

5. FBIHMJ
   - A. 518274
   - B. 152874
   - C. 528164
   - D. 517842

   5.____

6. MIHFQB
   - A. 872341
   - B. 782531
   - C. 782341
   - D. 783214

   6.____

7. JLFHQIM
   - A. 465237
   - B. 456387
   - C. 4652387
   - D. 4562387

   7.____

8. LBJQIFH
   - A. 614382
   - B. 6134852
   - C. 61437852
   - D. 61431852

   8.____

KEY (CORRECT ANSWERS)

1. C
2. A
3. D
4. B
5. A
6. B
7. C
8. A

TEST 2

DIRECTIONS: Each question or incomplete statement is followed by several suggested answers or completions. Select the one that BEST answers the question or completes the statement. *PRINT THE LETTER OF THE CORRECT ANSWER IN THE SPACE AT THE RIGHT.*

Questions 1-5.

DIRECTIONS: Questions 1 through 5 are based on the following list showing the name and number of each of nine inmates.

1.	Johnson	4.	Thompson	7.	Gordon
2.	Smith	5.	Frank	8.	Porter
3.	Edwards	6.	Murray	9.	Lopez

Each question consists of 3 sets of numbers and letters. Each set should consist of the numbers of three inmates and the first letter of each of their names. The letters should be in the same order as the numbers. In at least two of the three choices, there will be an error. On your answer sheet, mark only that choice in which the letters correspond with the numbers and are in the same order. If all three sets are wrong, mark choice D in your answer space.

SAMPLE QUESTION
A. 386 EPM
B. 542 FST
C. 474 LGT

Since 3 corresponds to E for Edwards, 8 corresponds to P for Porter, and 6 corresponds to M for Murray, choice A is correct and should be entered in your answer space. Choice B is wrong because letters T and S have been reversed. Choice C is wrong because the first number, which is 4, does NOT correspond with the first letter of choice C, which is L. It should have been T. If choice A were also wrong, then D would be the correct answer.

1. A. 382 EGS   B. 461 TMJ   C. 875 PLF   1.____

2. A. 549 FLT   B. 692 MJS   C. 758 GSP   2.____

3. A. 936 LEM   B. 253 FSE   C. 147 JTL   3.____

4. A. 569 PML   B. 716 GJP   C. 842 PTS   4.____

5. A. 356 FEM   B. 198 JPL   C. 637 MEG   5.____

Questions 6-10.

DIRECTIONS: Questions 6 through 10 are to be answered on the basis of the following information:

2 (#3)

In order to make sure stock is properly located, incoming units are stored as follows:

STOCK NUMBERS	BIN NUMBERS
00100 – 39999	D30, L44
40000 – 69999	14L, D38
70000 – 99999	41L, 80D
100000 and over	614, 83D

Using the above table, choose the answer A, B, C, or D, which lists the correct Bin Number for the Stock Number given.

6. 17243
   A. 41L   B. 83D   C. 14L   D. D30   6._____

7. 9219
   A. D38   B. L44   C. 614   D. 41L   7._____

8. 90125
   A. 41L   B. 614   C. D38   D. D30   8._____

9. 10001
   A. L44   B. D38   C. 80D   D. 83D   9._____

10. 200100
    A. 41L   B. 14L   C. 83D   D. D30   10._____

KEY (CORRECT ANSWERS)

1.	B	6.	D
2.	D	7.	B
3.	A	8.	A
4.	C	9.	A
5.	C	10.	C

TEST 3

DIRECTIONS: Each question or incomplete statement is followed by several suggested answers or completions. Select the one that BEST answers the question or completes the statement. *PRINT THE LETTER OF THE CORRECT ANSWER IN THE SPACE AT THE RIGHT.*

Questions 1-9.

DIRECTIONS: Assume that the Police Department is planning to conduct a statistical study of individuals who have been convicted of crimes during a certain year. For the purpose of this study, identification numbers are being assigned to individuals in the following manner:

The first two digits indicate the age of the individual.
The third digit indicates the sex of the individual:
    1. Male
    2. Female
The fourth digit indicates the type of crime involved:
    1. criminal homicide
    2. forcible rape
    3. robbery
    4. aggravated assault
    5. burglary
    6. larceny
    7. auto theft
    8. other
The fifth and sixth digits indicate the month in which the conviction occurred:
    01.   January
    02.   February, etc.

Questions 1 through 9 are to be answered SOLELY on the basis of the above information and the following list of individuals and identification numbers.

Name	Number	Name	Number
Abbott, Richard	271304	Morris, Chris	212705
Collins, Terry	352111	Owens, William	231412
Elders, Edward	191207	Parker, Leonard	291807
George, Linda	182809	Robinson, Charles	311102
Hill, Leslie	251702	Sands, Jean	202610
Jones, Jackie	301106	Smith, Michael	42108
Lewis, Edith	402406	Turner, Donald	191601
Mack, Helen	332509	White, Barbara	242803

1. The number of women on the above list is
   A. 6   B. 7   C. 8   D. 9

1.____

2. The two convictions which occurred during February were for the crimes of
   A. aggravated assault and auto theft
   B. auto theft and criminal homicide
   C. burglary and larceny
   D. forcible rape and robbery

   2._____

3. The ONLY man convicted of auto theft was
   A. Richard Abbott   B. Leslie Hill
   C. Chris Morris   D. Leonard Parker

   3._____

4. The number of people on the list who were 25 years old or older is
   A. 6   B. 7   C. 8   D. 9

   4._____

5. The OLDEST person on the list is
   A. Terry Collins   B. Edith Lewis
   C. Helen Mack   D. Michael Smith

   5._____

6. The two people on the list who are the same age are
   A. Richard Abbott and Michael Smith
   B. Edward Elders and Donald Turner
   C. Linda George and Helen Mack
   D. Leslie Hill and Charles Robinson

   6._____

7. A 28-year-old man who was convicted of aggravated assault in October would have identification number
   A. 281410   B. 281509   C. 282311   D. 282409

   7._____

8. A 33-year-old woman convicted in April of criminal homicide would have identification number
   A. 331140   B. 331204   C. 332014   D. 332104

   8._____

9. The number of people on the above list who were convicted during the first six months of the year is
   A. 6   B. 7   C. 8   D. 9

   9._____

Questions 10-19.

DIRECTIONS: The following is a list of patients who were referred by various clinics to the laboratory for tests. After each name is a patient identification number. Questions 10 through 19 are to be answered on the basis of the information contained in this list and the explanation accompanying it.

The first digit refers to the clinic which made the referral:
1. cardiac
2. Renal
3. Pediatrics
4. Ophthalmology
5. Orthopedics
6. Hematology
7. Gynecology
8. Neurology
9. Gastroenterology

3 (#2)

The second digit refers to the sex of the patient:
   1. male
   2. female
The third and fourth digits give the age of the patient
The last two digits give the day of the month the laboratory tests were performed

LABORATORY REFERRALS DURING JANUARY

Adams, Jacqueline	320917	Miller, Michael	511806
Black, Leslie	813406	Pratt, William	214411
Cook, Marie	511616	Rogers, Ellen	722428
Fisher, Pat	914625	Saunders, Sally	310229
Jackson, Lee	923212	Wilson, Jan	416715
James, Linda	624621	Wyatt, Mark	321326
Lane, Arthur	115702		

10. According to the list, the number of women referred to the laboratory during January was
    A. 4   B. 5   C. 6   D. 7

11. The clinic from which the MOST patients were referred was
    A. Cardiac   B. Gynecology
    C. Ophthalmology   D. Pediatrics

12. The YOUNGEST patient referred from any clinic other than Pediatrics was
    A. Leslie Black   B. Marie Cook
    C. Arthur Lane   D. Sally Saunders

13. The number of patients whose laboratory tests were performed on or before January 16 was
    A. 7   B. 8   C. 9   D. 10

14. The number of patients referred for laboratory tests who are under age 45 is
    A. 7   B. 8   C. 9   D. 10

15. The OLDEST patient referred to the clinic during January was
    A. Jacqueline Adams   B. Linda James
    C. Arthur Lane   D. Jan Wilson

16. The ONLY patient treated in the Orthopedics clinic was
    A. Marie Cook   B. Pat Fisher
    C. Ellen Rogers   D. Jan Wilson

17. A woman, age 37 was referred from the Hematology clinic to the laboratory. Her laboratory tests were performed on January 9.
    Her identification number would be
    A. 610937   B. 623709   C. 613790   D. 623790

18. A man was referred for lab tests from the Orthopedics clinic. He is 30 years old and his tests were performed on January 6.
His identification number would be
   A. 413006   B. 510360   C. 513006   D. 513060

18._____

19. A 4-year-old boy was referred from the Pediatrics clinic to have laboratory tests on January 23.
His identification number was
   A. 310422   B. 310423   C. 310433   D. 320403

19._____

KEY (CORRECT ANSWERS)

1.	B	11.	D
2.	B	12.	B
3.	B	13.	A
4.	D	14.	C
5.	D	15.	D
6.	B	16.	A
7.	A	17.	B
8.	D	18.	C
9.	C	19.	B
10.	B		

TEST 4

DIRECTIONS: Each question or incomplete statement is followed by several suggested answers or completions. Select the one that BEST answers the question or completes the statement. *PRINT THE LETTER OF THE CORRECT ANSWER IN THE SPACE AT THE RIGHT.*

Questions 1-10.

DIRECTIONS: Questions 1 through 10 are to be answered on the basis of the information and directions given below.

Assume that you are a Senior Stenographer assigned to the personnel bureau of a city agency. Your supervisor has asked you to classify the employees in your agency into the following five groups:

- A. Employees who are college graduates, who are at least 35 years of age but less than 50, and who have been employed by the City for five years or more;
- B. Employees who have been employed by the City for less than five years, who are not college graduates, and who earn at least $32,500 a year but less than $34,500;
- C. Employees who have been City employees for five years or more, who are at least 21 years of age but less than 35, and who are not college graduates;
- D. Employee who earn at least $34,500 a year but less than $36,000 who are college graduates, and who have been employed by the City for less than five years;
- E. Employees who are not included in any of the foregoing groups.

NOTE: In classifying these employees you are to compute age and period of service as of January 1, 2003. In all cases, it is to be assumed that each employee has been employed continuously in City service. In each question, consider only the information which will assist you in classifying each employee Any information which is of no assistance in classifying an employee would not be considered.

SAMPLE: Mr. Brown, a 29-year-old veteran, was appointed to his present position of Clerk on June 1, 2000. He has completed two years of college. His present salary is $33,050.

The correct answer to this sample is B, since the employee has been employed by the City for less than five years, is not a college graduate, and earn at least $32,500 a year but less than $34,500.

Questions 1 through 10 contain excerpts from the personnel records of 10 employees in the agency. In the correspondingly numbered space at the right print the capital letter preceding the appropriate group into which you would place each employee.

1. Mr. James has been employed by the City since 1993, when he was graduated from a local college. Now 35 years of age, he earns $36,000 a year.   1.____

2. Mr. Worth began working in City service early in 1999. He was awarded his college degree in 1994, at the age of 21. As a result of a recent promotion, he now earns $34,500 a year.   2.____

2 (#4)

3. Miss Thomas has been a City employee since August 1, 1998. Her salary is $34,500 a year. Miss Thomas, who is 25 years old, has had only three years of high school training.   3._____

4. Mr. Williams has had three promotions since entering City service on January 1, 1991. He was graduated from college with honors in 1974, when he was 20 years of age. His present salary is $37,000 a year.   4._____

5. Miss Jones left college after two years of study to take an appointment to a position in the City service paying $33,300 a year. She began work on March 1, 1997 when she was 19 years of age.   5._____

6. Mr. Smith was graduated from an engineering college with honors in January 1998 and became a City employee three months later. His present salary is $35,810. Mr. Smith was born in 1976.   6._____

7. Miss Earnest was born on May 31, 1979. Her education consisted of four years of high school and one year of business school. She was appointed as a typist in a City agency on June 1, 1997. Her annual salary is $33,500.   7._____

8. Mr. Adams, a 24-year-old clerk, began his City service on July 1, 1999, soon after being discharged from the U.S. Army. A college graduate, his present annual salary is $33,200.   8._____

9. Miss Charles attends college in the evenings, hoping to obtain her degree is 2004, when she will be 30 years of age. She has been a City employee since April 1998, and earns $33,350.   9._____

10. Mr. Dolan was just promoted to his present position after six years of City service. He was graduated from high school in 1982, when he was 18 years of age, but did not go on to college. Mr. Dolan's present salary is $33,500.   10._____

KEY (CORRECT ANSWERS)

1.	A	6.	D
2.	D	7.	C
3.	E	8.	E
4.	A	9.	B
5.	C	10.	E

TEST 5

DIRECTIONS: Questions 1 through 4 each contain five numbers that should be arranged in numerical order. The number with the lowest numerical value should be first and the number with the highest numerical value should be last. Pick that option which indicates the CORRECT order of the numbers.

Examples: A. 9; 18; 14; 15; 27
B. 9; 14; 15; 18; 27
C. 14; 15; 18; 27; 9
D. 9; 14; 15; 27; 18

The correct answer is B, which contains the proper arrangement of the five numbers.

1. A. 20573; 20753; 20738; 20837; 20098
   B. 20098; 20753; 20573; 20738; 20837
   C. 20098; 20573; 20753; 20837; 20738
   D. 20098; 20573; 20738; 20753; 20837

1.____

2. A. 113492; 113429; 111314; 113114; 131413
   B. 111314; 113114; 113429; 113492; 131413
   C. 111314; 113429; 113492; 113114; 131413
   D. 111314; 113114; 131413; 113429; 113492

2.____

3. A. 1029763; 1030421; 1035681; 1036928; 1067391
   B. 1030421; 1029763; 1035681; 1067391; 1036928
   C. 1030421; 1035681; 1036928; 1067391; 1029763
   D. 1029763; 1039421; 1035681; 1067391; 1036928

3.____

4. A. 1112315; 1112326; 1112337; 1112349; 1112306
   B. 1112306; 1112315; 1112337; 1112326; 1112349
   C. 1112306; 1112315; 1112326; 1112337; 1112349
   D. 1112306; 1112326; 1112315; 1112337; 1112349

4.____

KEY (CORRECT ANSWERS)

1. D
2. B
3. A
4. C

TEST 6

DIRECTIONS: The phonetic filing system is a method of filing names in which the alphabet is reduced to key code letters. The six key letters and their equivalents are as follows:

KEY LETTERS	EQUIVALENTS
b	p, f, v
c	s, k, g, j, q, x, z
d	t
l	none
m	n
r	none

A key letter represents itself.
Vowels (a, e, i, o, and u) and the letters w, h, and y are omitted.
For example, the name GILMAN would be represented as follows:
  G is represented by the key letter C.
  I is a vowel and is omitted.
  L is a letter and represents itself.
  M is a key letter and represents itself.
  A is a vowel and is omitted.
  N is represented by the key letter M.

Therefore, the phonetic filing code for the name GILMAN is CLMM.

Answer Questions 1 through 10 based on the information below.

1. The phonetic filing code for the name FITZGERALD would be
   A. BDCCRLD   B. BDCRLD   C. BDZCRLD   D. BTZCRLD

2. The phonetic filing code CLBR may represent any one of the following names EXCEPT
   A. Calprey   B. Flower   C. Glover   D. Silver

3. The phonetic filing code LDM may represent any one of the following names EXCEPT
   A. Halden   B. Hilton   C. Walton   D. Wilson

4. The phonetic filing code for the name RODRIGUEZ would be
   A. RDRC   B. RDRCC   C. RDRCZ   D. RTRCC

5. The phonetic filing code for the name MAXWELL would be
   A. MCLL   B. MCWL   C. MCWLL   D. MXLL

6. The phonetic filing code for the name ANDERSON would be
   A. AMDRCM   B. ENDRSM   C. MDRCM   D. NDERCN

7. The phonetic filing code for the name SAVITSKY would be
   A. CBDCC   B. CBDCY   C. SBDCC   D. SVDCC

109

2 (#6)

8. The phonetic filing code CMC may represent any one of the following names EXCEPT 8.____
   A. James   B. Jayes   C. Johns   D. Jones

9. The ONLY one of the following names that could be represented by the phonetic filing code CDDDM would be 9.____
   A. Catalano   B. Chesterton   C. Cittadino   D. Cuttlerman

10. The ONLY one of the following names that could be represented by the phonetic filing code LLMCM would be 10.____
    A. Ellington   B. Hallerman   C. Inslerman   D. Willingham

KEY (CORRECT ANSWERS)

1. A   6. C
2. B   7. A
3. D   8. B
4. B   9. C
5. A   10. D

GLOSSARY OF MEDICAL TERMS

Contents

	Page
ABCESS ...... BLOOD GROUPING	1
BLOOD CHEMISTRY ...... CYSTITIS	2
DIABETES (MELLITUS) ...... EPILEPSY	3
FURUNCLE (BOIL) ...... HEMATOMA	4
HEMORRHAGE (BLEEDING) ...... KIDNEY FAILURE (RENAL FAILURE)	5
LABORATORY PROCEDURES ...... METASTASIS	6
MULTIPLE SCLEROSIS ...... PARKINSONISM (PARALYSIS AGITANS)	7
PELLAGRA ...... PSORIASIS	8
PULMONARY EDEMA ...... SPASTIC PARALYSIS (CEREBRAL PALSY)	9
STROKE (CEREBRAL APOPLEXY) ...... VARICOSE VEINS	10

GLOSSARY OF MEDICAL TERMS

A

ABSCESS
Collection of pus in a tissue cavity resulting from a localized infection associated with cellular disintegration.

ALLERGY
Hypersensitive state stemming from exposure to a substance foreign to the body or to a physical agent (allergen) following a first contact. Subsequential exposure produces a reaction far more intense than the first one and entirely different.

ANEMIA
Decrease in the number of circulating red blood cells or in their hemoglobin (oxygen-carrying pigment) content. Can result from excessive bleeding or blood destruction (either inherited or disease caused) or from decreased blood formation (either nutritional deficiency or disease).

ANGINA
Choking pain. Angina pectoris: chest pain resulting from insufficient blood circulation through the hear vessels (coronaries), precipiated by exertion or emotion and usually relieved by a vasodilator drug.

ARTERIOSCLEROSIS
Generalized thickening, loss of elasticity, and hardening of the body's small and medium-size arteries.

ASTHMA
Disease characterized by repeated attacks of breath shortness, with wheezing, cough, and choking feeling due to a spasmodic narrowing of the small bronchi (small air tubes opening into the lung respiratory alveoli or cavities).

B

BIOPSY
Removal of a small piece of tissue or organ from the living body for microscopic or chemical examination to assist in disease diagnosis.

BRONCHITIS
Inflammation of the bronchi (tubular passages leading to lung cavities). It may be acute or chronic and caused by infection or the action of physical or chemical agents.

    BLOOD COUNT
        See: LABORATORY PROCEDURES

    BLOOD GROUPING
        See: LABORATORY PROCEDURES

2

BLOOD CHEMISTRY
  See: LABORATORY PROCEDURES

BLOOD CULTURE
  See: LABORATORY PROCEDURES

<u>C</u>

CANCER (NEOPLASM)
  A cellular tumor (swelling) resulting from uncontrolled tissue growth. Its natural evolution is to spread locally and to other body locations through the blood and lymph stream.

CATARACT
  Opacity of the normally transparent eye lens; this condition leads to impaired vision and stems from hereditary, nutritional, inflammatory, toxic, traumatic, or degenerative causes.

CATHETERIZATION
  Introduction of a narrow tubular instrument called a catheter into a body cavity to withdraw liquids (usually into the bladder for urine withdrawal).

CEREBROSPINAL FLUID EXAMINATION
  Chemical, microscopic, and bacteriological examination of a sample of the usually clear and colorless liquid bathing the brain and spinal cord. The sample is usually removed by needle puncture of the lumbar spine.

CIRRHOSIS
  Chronic liver ailment, characterized by an increase in its fibrous support tissue that results in a progressive destruction of liver cells and impairment of the organ's function.

CONJUNCTIVITIS
  Acute or chronic inflammation of the conjuctiva the delicate transparent membrane lining the eyelids and covering the exposed surface of the eyeball. It results from the action of bacteria, allergens, and physical or chemical irritants.

CYST
  Any normal or abnormal sac in the body, especially one containing a liquid or semiliquid material.

CYSTIC FIBROSIS
  An inherited disease of the glands of external secretion, affecting mostly the pancreas, respiratory tract, and sweat glands. It usually manifests itself in infancy.

CYSTITIS
  Acute or chronic inflammation of the urinary bladder, caused by infection or irritation from foreign bodies (kidney stones) or chemicals. Its symptoms are frequent voiding accompanied by burning sensation

D

DIABETES (MELLITUS)
Hereditary or acquired disorder in which there is a sugar-utilization deficiency in the body, caused by an absolute or relative insufficiency of the normal internal secretion of the pancreas (insulin). Symptoms are thirst, hunger, itching, weakness, and increased frequency of urination. Diabetes can be controlled by diet drugs, or the administration of insulin. Lack of treatment leads to various complications, including death.

E

ECZEMA
Inflammatory skin disease that produces a great variety of lesions, such as vesicles, thickening of skin, watery discharge, and scales and crusts, with itching and burning sensations. Eczema is caused by allergy, infections, and nutritional, physical, and sometimes unknown factors.

EDEMA
Excessive accumulation of water and salt in the tissue spaces, caused by kidney or heart disease (generalized edema) or by local circulatory impairment stemming from inflammation, trauma, or neoplasm (localized edema).

ELECTROCARDIOGRAM (ECG or EKG)
Graphic tracing of the electric current that is produced by the rhythmic contraction of the heart muscle. Visually, a periodic wave pattern is produced. Changes in the wave pattern may appear in the course of various heart diseases; the tracing is obtained by applying electrodes on the skin of the chest and limbs.

ELECTROENCEPHALOGRAM (EEG)
Graphic recording of the electric current created by the activity of the brain. The electrodes are placed on the scalp. It is used in the diagnosis of organic brain disease.

EMBOLISM
Sudden blocking of an artery by a dislodged blood clot (after surgery), a fat globule (after a fracture), gas bubbles (after sudden decompression), bacterial clumps (bacterial endocarditis), or other foreign matter. The arteries most usually affected are those of the brain, heart, lungs, and extremities.

EMPHYSEMA
Lung disease characterized by overdistention of the chest and destruction of the walls separating the lung air sacs (alveoli). It results in a reduction of the respiratory surface, chronic shortness of breath, wheezing, and cough.

EPILEPSY
Disease characterized by sudden and brief attacks of convulsions, which are associated with impairment or loss of consciousness, psychic or sensory disturbances, and autonomic nervous system perturbations. Epilepsy causes the EEG to show characteristic brain wave alterations.

F

FURUNCLE (BOIL)
Acute and painful infection of the skin surrounding a hair root. Its center contains pus and dead tissue (core) that has to be discharged either spontaneously or surgically for proper cure.

G

GANGRENE
Localized tissue death, following interruption of the blood supply to the area; gangrene is associated with bacterial infection and putrefaction.

GASTRITIS
Acute or chronic inflammation of the lining of the stomach. It may be caused by the ingestion of alcohol, spices, medicines, chemicals, foods, as well as by infections or allergy.

GASTROSCOPY
Diret visualization of the stomach interior by means of an optical instrument called a gastroscope.

GASTROINTESTINAL SERIES (G.I. SERIES)
Serial X-ray examination of the stomach and intestines to detect, organic or functional alterations, enabling proper diagnosis and treatment of disease.

GLAUCOMA
Eye disease characterized by an increase in its internal pressure, caused by alteration of the intra-ocular fluid flow, and resulting in visual impairment, and if untreated, blindness.

GOITER
Enlargement of the thyroid gland that shows as a well-defined swelling at the base of the neck. Goiter is usually associated with iodine deficiency (endemic goiter), or with excessive secretion of thyroid hormones (exopthalmic goiter).

GOUT
A disturbance of body chemistry, manifested by elevated uric acid blood levels and excessive deposits in tissues, particularly joints and cartilages. It is characterized by repeated attacks of acute and very painful inflammation of joints, especially those of the big toe but also of ankles, knees, wrists, and elbows.

H

HEMATOMA
Swelling produced by a collection of blood escaping from a ruptured blood vessel, resulting from trauma or injury. It is generally located under the skin and subcutaneous tissue, or under the bony structure of the skull.

HEMORRHAGE (BLEEDING)
Any copious blood loss from the circulation. If sufficently severe or unchecked, it may lead to anemia or shock.

HEMORRHOIDS (PILES)
Abnormal dilation of the veins of the rectum and anus, causing local swelling, pain, itching, bleeding, and induration.

HEPATITIS
Liver inflammation, caused by infection or toxics. It is characterized by jaundice (yellow coloration of skin and membranes, especially of the eye) and is usually accompanied by fever and other disease manifestations.

HERNIA
Protrusion of a portion of an organ or tissue through an abnormal body opening. Inguinal hernia is one of the most common and consists of an intestinal loop protruding at the groin.

HYPERTENSION
Disease characterized by elevated blood pressure, resulting from the functional or pathological narrowing of the peripheral small arteries. Except in limited instances, its cause is generally unknown.

I

INFARCT
A circumscribed portion of tissue which has suddenly been deprived of its blood supply by embolism or thrombosis and which, as a result, is undergoing death (necrosis), to be replaced by scar tissue.

INFARCTION
The formation of an infarct; an infarct.

INTESTINAL OBSTRUCTION
Blocking of the normal flow of the intestinal contents, caused by twisting of a gut loop, benign tumor, cancer, or foreign body.

INTRADERMAL INJECTION
Injection into the skin proper. It is used less than hypodermic injection, which is done into the loose subcutaneous (under the skin) tissue.

K

KIDNEY FAILURE (RENAL FAILURE)
Severe reduction or impairment of the excretory function of the kidney. The acute form occurs most frequently after crushing injuries, transfusion of mismatched blood, severe burns or shock, generalized infections, obstetric accidents, and certain chemical poisoning.

L

LABORATORY PROCEDURES
Laboratory tests performed to assist in disease diagnosis and treatment, Usually these tests are carried out on samples of blood, urine, or other body fluids.

The MOST common are:

Blood Count
Determination of the number and percentage of red and white blood cells from a blood sample that is obtained by puncturing a vein or the skin. It consists of a red blood cell count (RBC), white blood count (WBC), and platelet count.

Blood Grouping
Blood typing for selecting and matching blood transfusion donors and for the diagnosis of various diseases.

Blood Chemistry
Determination of the content of various blood chemicals; the most usual are: sugar, for diabetes; urea nitrogen (BUN), for kidney or liver disease; uric acid, for gout; and cholesterol, for vascular and liver disease.

Blood Culture
Investigation to detect the presence of pathogenic germs by special culturing in artificial media.

Urinalysis (Urine Analysis)
Examination of urine constituents, both normal (urea, uric acid, total nitrogen, ammonia, chlorides, phosphate, and others) and abnormal (albumin, glucose, acetone, bile, blood, cells, and bacteria).

M

MENINGITIS
Inflammation of the enveloping membranes of the brain or spinal cord, caused by virus, bacteria, yeasts, fungi, or protozoa. It is a serious disease and may be a complication of another bodily infection.

METABOLISM
The total of the physical and chemical processes occuring in the living organism by which its substance is produced, maintained, and exchanged with transformation of energy; this energy itself provides fuel for all body functions and heat production.

METASTASIS
Transfer of a disease (usually cancer) from one part of the body to another that is not immediately connected with it.

MULTIPLE SCLEROSIS
A chronic and slowly progressive disease of unknown cause that is characterized by patches of fibrous tissue degeneration in brain and spinal cord, causing various nervous system symptoms; the disease's course is marked by occasional periods of worsening or improvement.

MUSCULAR DYSTROPHY
An inherited disease that involves the progressive weakness and degeneration of voluntary skeletal muscle fibers without nerve involvement.

MYOCARDITIS
Inflammation of the heart muscle that is associated with or caused by a number of infectious diseases, toxic chemicals, drugs and traumatic agents.

MYOCARDIUM
The muscular substance of the heart; adj., myocardial.

N

NEPHRITIS
Inflammatory, acute or chronic disease of the kidneys, which usually follows some form of infection or toxic chemical poisoning. It impairs renal function, causing headache, dropsy, elevated blood pressure, and appearance of albumin in urine.

NEURALGIA
Brief attach of acute and severe shooting pain along the course of one or more peripheral nerves, usually with clear cause.

NEURITIS
Inflammation or degeneration of one or more peripheral nerves, causing pain, tenderness, tingling, sensations, numbness, paralysis, muscle weakness, and wasting and disappearance of reflexes in the area involved. The cause may be infectious, toxic, nutritional (vitamin Bl deficiency), or unknown.

P

PANCREATITIS
Inflammation of the pancreas, either mild or acute, and fulminating. The chronic form is characterized by recurrent attacks of diverse severity. Symptoms are sudden abdominal pain, tenderness and distention, vomiting and, in severe cases, shock and circulatory collapse.

PAP SMEARS (PAPANICOLAU SMEARS)
Method of staining smears of various body secretions -- especially vaginal but also respiratory, digestive, or genitourinary -- to detect cancer by examining the normally shed cells in the smear. The procedure is named for its developer.

PARKINSONISM (PARALYSIS AGITANS)
A usually chronic condition, marked by muscular rigidity, immobile face, excessive salivation, and tremor. These symptoms characterize Parkinson's disease; however, they are also observed in the course of treatment with psycho-pharmaceutical drugs or following encephalitis or trauma.

PELLAGRA
A disease caused by a vitamin (niacin) deficiency and characterized by skin, alimentary tract, and nervous system disturbances.

PERICARDITIS
Acute or chronic inflammation of the pericardium (fibrous sac surrounding the heart), caused by infection, trauma, myocardial infarction, cancer, or complication from other diseases.

PERITONITIS
Acute or chronic inflammation of the serous membrane lining abdominal walls and covering the contained viscerae. Its symptoms are abdominal pain and tenderness, nausea, vomiting, moderate fever, and constipation. It is usually caused by infectious agents or foreign matter entering the abdominal cavity from the intestinal tract (perforation), female genital tract, blood dissemination, or the outside (wounds, surgery).

PERNICIOUS ANEMIA
A chronic anemia, characterized by gastrointestinal and neurological disturbances that usually occur in late adult life and are caused by a deficiency (B12).

PHLEBITIS
Condition caused by inflammation of a vein wall, resulting in the formation of a blood clot inside its cavity. Phlebitis produces pain, swelling, and stiffness of the affected part, generally a limb.

PLEURISY
Acute or chronic inflammation of the pleura (serous membrane lining the thoracic cavity and lungs). It often accompanies inflammatory lung diseases and may be caused by infection (tuberculous, viral or other), cancer, or cardiac infarction. Symptoms are stabbing pain in the thorax, aggravated by respiratory movements and shortness of breath.

PNEUMONIA
An acute inflammation or infection of the lung, caused by bacteria or virus. Chills, sharp chest pain, shortness of breath, cough, rusty sputum, fever, and headache are primary symptoms.

PNEUMOTHORAX
Accumulation of air or gas in the pleural cavity (between the chest wall and the lung), resulting in lung collapse. It may be spontaneous, following a penetrating chest wound or some diseases, or may be deliberately induced for treatment of lung ailments (tuberculosis).

POLYP
A protruding excrescence or growth from a mucous membrane, usually of the nasal passages but also of the uterine cervix, alimentary tract, or vocal cords.

PSORIASIS
Chronic, occasionally acute, recurrent skin disease of unknown cause, characterized by thickened red skin patches that are covered with whitish shiny scales. Psoriasis usually affects the scalp, elbows, knees, back, and buttocks.

PULMONARY EDEMA
Usually an acute condition in which there is a waterlogging of the lung tissue, including its alveolar cavities. Respiration is impaired. If inadequately treated, it may lead to rapid death; it is often a complication of chronic heart disease.

R

RHEUMATIC FEVER
Disease characterized by initial sore throat, chills, high fever, and painful inflammation of large joints. Frequently cardiac complications follow, leading to permanent organic heart disease.

RICKETS
Generally a disease of infants and young children caused by a vitamin D deficiency. There is defective bone calcification that causes skeletal deformities, such as bow legs, knock knees, and pigeon chest.

S

SCIATICA
A severe pain along the sciatic nerve, which extends from the buttocks along the back of the thigh and leg to the ankle. It is caused by mechanical pressure on the nerve at its spinal origin (from injury, local disease, or tumors).

SCOLIOSIS
A marked lateral curvature of the normally straight vertical spine, which may be caused by disease or mechanical deviation of the bones or muscles of the spine, hips, or legs.

SEPTICEMIA
Presence of bacteria or bacterial toxins in the circulating blood. This condition results from breakdown of local defenses, permitting the spread of a circumscribed infection to the bloodstream and rest of the body.

SILICOSIS
Occupational disease, usually chronic, causing fibrosis of the lungs. It results from inhalation of the dust of stone, flint, or sand that contains silica (quartz). Called "grinders* disease," it is observed in workers who have breathed such dust over a period of five to 25 years.

SLIPPED DISK
An acute or chronic condition, caused by the traumatic or degenerative displacement and protrusion of the softened central core of an intervertebral disk (cartilagenous disk between the spine bones), especially of the lower back. Symptoms are low back pain, which frequently extends to the thigh; muscle spasm; and tenderness.

SPASTIC PARALYSIS (CEREBRAL PALSY)
A condition probably stemming from various causes present since birth. Associated with nonprogressive brain damage, cerebral palsy is characterized by spastic, jerky voluntary movements, or constant involuntary and irregular writhing motion.

STROKE (CEREBRAL APOPLEXY)
A sudden attack of paralysis, with disturbance of speech and thought. It is caused by the destruction of brain substance, as the result of brain hemorrhage, vascular damage, intravascular clotting, or local circulatory insufficiency.

T

THROMBOPHLEBITIS
Condition caused by the inflammation of a vein complicated by the formation of an intravascular blood clot (thrombus). Circulation is obstructed in the affected area, usually the legs.

THROMBOSIS
Formation, development, or presence of a blood clot inside an artery or vein. This condition can be serious, if it affects the blood vessels of vital organs, such as the brain, heart, or lungs.

TUMOR
A swelling or growth of new tissue; it develops independently of surrounding structures and serves no specific function of its own.

U

UREMIA
Toxic clinical condition, caused by renal insufficiency resulting in the retention of urinary waste products in the circulating blood.

URINANALYSIS
See: LABORATORY PROCEDURES

V

VARICOSE VEINS
Abnormally distended and lengthened superficial veins caused by slowing and obstruction of the normal blood backflow. Varicose veins are most commonly observed in the legs, anus and rectum (hemorrhoids), and scrotum (varicocele).